The Royal Governors of Georgia

The Institute of Early American History and Culture is sponsored jointly by the College of William and Mary and Colonial Williamsburg, Incorporated. Publication of this book has been assisted by a grant from the Lilly Endowment, Incorporated.

The Royal Governors
of Georgia ᨀ 1754-1775

By *W. W. ABBOT*

PUBLISHED FOR THE

Institute of Early American History and Culture

AT WILLIAMSBURG

BY

The University of North Carolina Press · Chapel Hill

Preface

A DECADE OR SO AGO I began a study of political developments in Georgia in the years after the formation of the federal union. As is often the case in such projects, I felt the need of knowing more of what went before if I were to proceed. Deciding to back up for a better start, I retreated to the beginning of Georgia's royal period, dug in, and began to work my way forward. Months became years, my notes piled higher and higher, and I had got no further in my investigations than the outbreak of the Revolution, still almost a quarter of a century short of the starting line. With one bird pretty well in hand I decided to be practical about the thing and write an account of pre-Revolutionary Georgia, leaving the other until later.

This little book is the consequence of the decision. It also helps to explain why I have spent five happy years in Williamsburg, where this manuscript was brought to the point of publication under the goading and encouragement of the department of history at the College of William and Mary and the staff of the Institute of Early American History and Culture. When the late Professor Charles S. Sydnor informed me that the college at Williamsburg was looking for a colonial historian, I was surprised and delighted to learn that was what I had become. I had not known before that there were different kinds, only American historians and the others who could do foreign languages and became European historians. I have clung to the designation and now that I am at last publishing a book of colonial history and teaching it as well, I feel a little less a pretender to what I am not.

What I attempt here is simply a study of developments in Georgia during its royal period, from 1754 to the Revolution. In 1752, the Trustees in London—who in 1733 had begun their experiment with colonization south of the Savannah River in North America—surrendered their charter to the king. The project had proved in many ways a failure: few more than two thousand white inhabitants, and most of these poverty-stricken, lived in Georgia. The first governor appointed by the king arrived late in 1754 and the last left early in 1776. Under the rule of the governors the colony quickly found its footing and went on to become in a short time a thriving and productive province of the British Empire. This era of material progress coincided with the great crisis in the Empire which led to its breakup and the eventual establishment of a separate American union. In the end Georgia joined her sisters in revolution and royal government disappeared.

This is my story and I have sought to tell it largely in terms of the royal governor and to regard developments from his vantage point. I have done so partly because most of the surviving records view the scene from the governor's position and partly because of a conviction that he is the key to the situation and the proper peg to hang the tale on.

The custodians of books and manuscripts I consulted were uniformly kind and helpful. Friends and colleagues have done much to make me see things in my story I should see and to leave off seeing things not there. Mrs. Lilla M. Hawes of the Georgia Historical Society Library made my long visits there both profitable and—with the help of Savannah, loveliest of towns—pleasant. The years spent working with and for Professor Sydnor at Duke University developed in me whatever insight into the doings of the past I might display in what follows. And my colleague on the *William and Mary*

Quarterly, always helpful with criticism and advice as Eleanor Pearre, has been invaluable as Eleanor Abbot.

I thank the University of Georgia Press for permission to use in part the essay I contributed to *Georgians in Profile*, edited by Horace Montgomery and published at Athens in 1958.

W.W.A.

Contents

The Royal Governors of Georgia

Augusta

Savannah River

SOUTH
CAROLINA

Ogeechee River

Charleston

GEORGIA

Beaufort

Ebenezer

Savannah
Fort Argyle

Tybee Island

Altamaha River

Sunbury

ATLANTIC OCEAN

Darien

N

St. Marys River

FLORIDA

St. Johns River

St. Augustine

0   25   50 MILES

ST. NEELY

CHAPTER I

Material Progress and Political Revolution, 1754-1775

IN LATE OCTOBER 1754 the first royal governor of Georgia, Captain John Reynolds, sailed past the crude lighthouse on Tybee Island into the river and on up to the capital of the colony at Savannah. Savannah was a desolate little town overlooking the river. A few hundred people lived there in frame dwellings. No wall or fortification stood between the houses and the pine forest which pressed in from three sides, cutting off the breeze from the sea on breathless summer days. Unprepossessing as it was, Savannah in 1754 was the one sizable settlement in the colony. Nearby Acton, Abercorn, and Vernonburgh were only names. To the south along the coast, Oglethorpe's Frederica was already deserted; the Scottish Highlanders' Darien was no more than a hamlet, and the newly arrived South Carolina Congregationalists had not yet built Sunbury. A short distance up the river from Savannah a congregation of Salzburgers lived in a place called Ebenezer, but Ebenezer was little more than a cluster of farm lots hemmed into the mud bottoms of the Savannah River and Ebenezer Creek by the ubiquitous pine barrens. The town of Augusta, about one hundred miles farther up the river, just below the fall line, consisted of a ramshackle fort used as an Indian trading post. For the rest, the forest lay undisturbed except here and there a clearing where a farmer with his family tilled the soil and during the winter months fed his livestock.

Between the Altamaha River and the mouth of the Savannah, Georgia claimed more than one hundred miles of marshy coastline partially shielded from the Atlantic by a chain of semitropical islands. The colony also included the western bank of the Savannah, the river which separates Georgia from South Carolina. This strip of land extended in a northwesterly direction for about 150 miles inland from Savannah to Augusta. The stretch of territory along the coast and up the river over which Reynolds assumed control, at first view extensive, was not as great as it seemed. The Indians, who had ceded only the tidelands along the coast, were extremely watchful for any white settlements "above the Flowing of the Tides." While keeping the whites within thirty miles of the sea, the Indians at the same time tied them almost as closely to the Savannah River. In all, the colony controlled only about eighteen hundred square miles of territory in 1754.[1]

The inhabitants of Georgia, strung out as they were for some three hundreds of miles, numbered hardly more than three thousand men, women, and children, black and white.[2] And few new settlers were coming in.[3] Of the seven or eight hundred white men living in the colony, a small number had begun

1. *The South-Carolina Gazette* (Charleston), Oct. 31, Nov. 14, 1754; Gov. John Reynolds to Board of Trade, Dec. 5, 1754, Jan. 5, 1756, unpublished Colonial Records (typescript copy deposited at Georgia Historical Society, Savannah), XXVII, 69-72, 237-43 (hereafter cited unpub. Col. Records); Lt. Gov. Henry Ellis to Board of Trade, Mar. 11, 1757, *ibid.*, XXVIII, Part 1, 4-15; John Gerar William De Brahm, *History of the Province of Georgia* (Wormsloe, Ga., 1849), 38-40, 45; "An Account of the Heat of the Weather in Georgia: In a Letter from His Excellency Henry Ellis, Esq., Governor of Georgia, and F. R. S. to John Ellis, Esq., F. R. S.," *The London Magazine* (1759), 371-72; An Exemplification of the Proceedings of Court between Our Sovereign Lord the King and Thomas Goldsmith at Savannah 28 Jany., 1754, Raymond Demeré Papers, Duke University Library, Durham; Reynolds to Loudoun, July 23, 1756, Jeffrey Amherst Papers, Library of Congress; Ellis to William Henry Lyttelton, Feb. 4, 1760, Lyttelton Papers, William L. Clements Library, Ann Arbor; Lt. Gov. James Wright to Board of Trade, Dec. 23, 1760, unpub. Col. Records, XXVIII, Part 1, 477-88; Reynolds to Lyttelton, Sept. 8, 1756, Lyttelton Papers, Clements Lib.

2. Reynolds to Board of Trade, Jan. 5, 1756, unpub. Col. Records, XXVII, 237-43; Reynolds to Loudoun, July 23, 1756, Amherst Papers, Lib. Cong.; Ellis to Loudoun, Feb. 28, 1757, *ibid.*

3. For instance in the first half of 1756 there were 63 new grants made, but all except 9 recipients have been identified as old settlers. Duplicates of Abstracts of Grants of Lands Registered in Georgia from 27th January to 27th July, 1756, unpub. Col. Records, XXVII, 301-26.

to build their fortunes by acquiring land suitable for rice cultivation along the rivers in the tidewater. Slavery had been allowed in the colony for only four years in 1754, but already
enterprising men were investing all of the capital and credit
they could scrape together in Negroes to work the rice fields.
A few had made connections in Charleston or in England for
importing goods which in a short time would make them
prosperous merchants. There were others who were artisans,
mechanics, clerks, and the like; but the vast majority were small
farmers subsisting on the livestock and food crops and game
which their farms and the adjacent woods afforded.

The farms of Georgia in the mid-fifties yielded little surplus
for export. The amount of rice, lumber, indigo, pork, and beef
being sent overseas from Savannah was only a fraction of what
it was to become in a few years. Although Savannah was a port
by virtue of its geographical location, the shipping which went
down the river from the town during Reynolds' time was negli-
gible. What surplus there was usually went by boat to creditors
in Charleston to be loaded there with the produce of South
Carolina.[4]

Georgia had remained small and unproductive largely because it had been unable to offer protection to its inhabitants.
In the fall of 1754, the fear of Indian attack hung like a pall
over the tiny colony. Thousands of Creek and Cherokee warriors, who could expect aid from the Spanish at St. Augustine
and the French at Mobile in any move to discomfit the English
settlers of Georgia, lived on the land to the north, to the west,
and to the south. Despite its obvious peril, Georgia was
practically defenseless. The colony was without usable fort or

4. The discussion of economic conditions in this chapter is based mainly on
the manuscript and printed records cited in footnote 8 and upon the letters
appearing on the following pages of the unpublished Colonial Records: XXVII,
77, 182-90, 259-63, 265; XXVIII, Part 1, 4-15, 16-17, 18-31, 42-45, 50-55,
57-60, 97-101, 171-73, 187-217, 252-56, 291-303, 511-16, 600-5, 647-50,
662-63; XXVIII, Part 2, 114-16, 407-12, 414-40, 560-77, 693-700, 706-10,
863-67; XXXIV, 162-70, 220-36; XXXVII, 206-12, 499-506, 565-68, 599-600,
651-53; XXXVIII, Part 1, 4-8, 38-39, 42-45, 158-60, 196-98; XXXIX, 10-15,
26-29.

fortification and had neither troops nor weapons. A few hundred militiamen, untrained, poorly armed, and for the most part ready to run away at the first sign of hostilities, stood between the colony and destruction. After twenty years of danger and toil, Georgia was still feebly struggling for its very existence.[5]

The Georgia of 1754 fell far short of the colony envisioned by the group of London magnates and philanthropists who secured its charter in 1732. Their motives for planting a colony on the frontier of South Carolina were mixed, but long before Governor Reynolds' arrival it had become clear that few if any of the conflicting aims and plans of the proprietors were being realized, or likely to be. Instead of an effective buffer for Carolina, Georgia in 1754 remained in some ways an added burden to the South Carolina military establishment. The silk and wine with which Georgia was to challenge the French monopoly had failed to materialize. Year after year unseasonable late frosts had blighted the grapevines and mulberry bushes of the early settlers. Nor had Georgia become a haven for the poor and oppressed of the world as some of the Trustees had hoped. The world's unfortunates seemingly found familiar hardships preferable to the prospect of living on an unprotected frontier infested with Indians, menaced by Spaniards, and plagued by fevers of the most virulent sort. No one "exempt from the terrors of a Jail" would come to such a place.[6] As time went by, the urgent necessity of enticing settlers to Georgia had forced the Trustees to abandon their attempt to impose certain estimable but unpopular restrictions on the new colony. A more or less communal ownership of land had been replaced with outright private ownership aimed at such rapid exploitation as was common in the other British colonies in the South. The forlorn hope that the new country could be kept

5. Reynolds to Board of Trade, Jan. 5, 1756, unpub. Col. Records, XXVII, 237-43; Wright to Board of Trade, Dec. 23, 1760, *ibid.*, XXVIII, Part 1, 477-88.
6. Ellis to Board of Trade, Mar. 11, 1757, *ibid.*, XXVIII, Part 1, 4-15.

free of troublesome lawyers and strong drink had been given up. And slavery had at last been made legal. But these concessions had come too late, and in 1752 the Trustees had handed over their sickly charge to the King.

In the autumn of 1754, the one ray of light in an otherwise gloomy picture was "the general face of Chearfulness" evident throughout the colony at the prospect of the imminent arrival of a royal governor.[7] The really remarkable growth in strength and wealth of Georgia during the next twenty years fully justified the citizenry's delight at being taken under the King's protection. The royal governors steered the colony clear of any real war with the neighboring savages during these crucial years, and the last of these, James Wright, was even able to prevail upon the Indians to cede from time to time a total of some six million acres of land. Although Savannah's enthusiastic welcome for the royal governor in 1754 had by 1775 become a fixed determination to be done with his services forever, the fact remains that it was largely through the efforts of the governors that Georgia weathered the perilous days when the survival of the colony hung in the balance of the Indians' intentions, and, by the time of the Revolution, the Indians had become as much a nuisance as a menace.

Under the leadership of the royal governors, Georgia grew prodigiously as its trade and production rapidly expanded.[8] Savannah developed into a thriving little town with wharves

7. *S. C. Gaz.*, Nov. 14, 1754.
8. Thomas Rasberry Letter Book, Aug. 9, 1758–Feb. 9, 1761, and Letter Book of Joseph Clay & Co., Apr. 11, 1774–May 16, 1776, Georgia Historical Society; Letter Book of Edward Telfair and Cowper & Telfair, Aug. 11, 1773–Aug. 9, 1775, and Letter Books of William & Edward Telfair & Co. and Edward Telfair & Co., Jan. 12, 1774–Dec. 24, 1776, Telfair Academy of Arts and Sciences, Savannah; Telfair Papers and Gibbons Papers, Duke University Library; *The Letters of Hon. James Habersham, 1756-1775*, Georgia Historical Society, *Collections*, VI (Savannah, 1904); the *Georgia Gazette* (Savannah), July 20, 1768, Sept. 20, Dec. 27, 1769, June 22, Oct. 5, 1774; *S. C. Gaz.*, Apr. 28, 1757, May 30, 1774; Allen D. Candler, ed., *The Colonial Records of the State of Georgia* (Atlanta, 1904-16), VII, 507; XIII, 84, 617 (hereafter cited *Col. Records*); "Report of Sir James Wright on the Condition of the Province of Georgia, on 20th Sept. 1773," Ga. Hist. Soc., *Colls.*, III (Savannah, 1873), 158-79; Ellis to Lyttelton, Apr. 1757, Lyttelton Papers, Clements Lib.

and storehouses lining the bluff. From 1766 to 1774 the tide was kept busy bringing up to the town ships loaded with foreign goods and then taking them down again to the sea, their holds filled with rice and other products of the province. Whereas only fifty-two ships were cleared from the port of Savannah in 1755, 161 vessels put to sea from Tybee Light and fifty-six from the new port at Sunbury in 1772. That same year, twenty-five seagoing vessels called Savannah or Sunbury their home port. In 1755 the weight of the cargo shipped from Savannah came to only 1,899 tons valued at about £16,000. Fifteen years later 10,514 tons of produce worth nearly £100,000 left Georgia bound for foreign ports.[9] Savannah soon boasted a coterie of prosperous merchants; by 1770 several rice planters in Georgia were numbering their slaves in the hundreds and counting their yearly income in thousands of pounds.[10]

The royal government of Georgia was frankly and effectively the partner of its constituents in their struggle for wealth and well-being. No effort was spared by the administration to bring new men in and, once they had come, to help them prosper. In all of this the royal governor was the prime mover, the key figure. He was the center of power in the provincial government. But his was a dual role. The governor was, on the one hand, the imperial representative of the British king in Georgia and, on the other, the chief magistrate of the colony itself. As the king's representative, he was expected to guard the interests of the Empire in the colony and to carry out the instructions sent him by the British government. The king was assured of the governor's first loyalty by the fact that most of his power was derived from the British government and not from the colonists: the king appointed him, Parliament paid his salary, and the prestige and might of the British Empire gave

9. De Brahm, *History of Georgia*, 52; Report of Sir James Wright, 1773, Ga. Hist. Soc., *Colls.*, III, 158-79.

10. Sir James Wright, James Habersham, and John Graham certainly belonged in this category.

him powers and functions independent of the vagaries of colonial politics. But he was, at the same time, the chief magistrate in the colony of Georgia with responsibilities and loyalties to it. As the leader of the colony, he had extensive powers that allowed him to direct the course it should follow.

In carrying out his instructions from home and in administering the affairs of the colony, the governor had the aid of several crown officers, chief of whom were the secretary, the chief justice, the attorney general, the provost marshal, and the surveyor general. These officers were appointed by the king and were often sent out from England. Although the governor, to his regret, had little voice in their selection, he did retain the power of suspension. He also appointed during pleasure all lesser officials, including justices of the peace and the three assistant judges of the general court.

The leading crown officers were usually members of the governor's Council, appointed by the king on the recommendation of the governor and subject to the governor's suspension. The Council, composed of from seven to twelve of the most substantial men in the province, was supposed to advise and aid the governor in the performance of his duties and to act as a check on him should he become arbitrary or unreasonable. During the time that the legislature was in session, the Council, sitting as an upper house, shared in the legislative process and came to be a bulwark on which the governor relied in opposing the recurrent attempts of the lower house to extend its powers.

The lower house, called the Commons House of Assembly, was elected by the colonists. Its powers and procedures, ultimately derived in a sense from the British House of Commons, were patterned immediately after its counterparts in the older royal colonies. Any attempt to deny the Georgia House of Assembly rights allowed the lower house of the legislature in South Carolina was cause for agitation and stubborn protest. The Commons House of Assembly in Georgia originally consisted of nineteen men elected in the various districts of the province; but, beginning in the summer of 1760, a total of twenty-five assemblymen were sent to Savannah from the newly created parishes. The Assembly had as its main task initiating legislation and representing to the governor and to the appropriate officials in London the needs and wishes of the colonists.

An election to choose new members of the Assembly was held whenever the governor ordered. At such times, the provost marshal sent writs to his deputies in the several districts or parishes giving them instructions and authority for holding an election. Each deputy then took a poll of the voters at the prescribed place and time. Any male white inhabitant past the age of twenty who owned fifty acres of land could vote, by voice, in the election. The poll taken, the deputy returned the completed writ to the marshal in Savannah. The Assembly reserved the right to review the writs and to judge the validity of the election of any of its members.[11]

In actual practice, of course, the individual elections varied greatly from place to place and from time to time. The first election, held in 1754, is a case in point. In the town and district of Savannah, this election was bitterly contested—in the weeks before it was held, at the poll, and finally on the floor of the House. Yet, in neighboring districts where the electorate was small and the voters' preferences well-known, the issue was in so little doubt that spokesmen for these districts were able to offer three seats to a gentleman from Savannah some time before formal polls were taken.[12] In the same election, in the Midway district to the south, the Congregationalists simply called a meeting of the Church members, chose the representative for the district, and forwarded his name to the marshal.[13]

The intense interest shown in the election of 1754 at Savan-

11. Reynolds' Commission and Instructions, unpub. Col. Records, XXXIV, 1-16, 24-82; Journal of the Commons House of Assembly, *Col. Records*, XIII-XV.

12. Joseph Ottolenghé to Benjamin Martin, Nov. 20, 30, 1754, unpub. Col. Records, XXVII, 86-90; Reynolds to Board of Trade, Feb. 28, 1755, *ibid.*, 126-29; Journal of Assembly, Jan. 9–Mar. 6, 1755, *Col. Records*, XIII, 9-77.

13. Midway Congregational Church Records, 1754-1788, Georgia Historical Society.

nah proved to be rather unusual. In 1769 and again in 1772, for instance, the four representatives of the town were elected without opposition.[14] Details of pre-election campaigning or electioneering by the candidates for seats in the royal legislature are hard to come by, but evidence that a man's friends were sometimes active in behalf of his candidacy is not lacking: the *Georgia Gazette* in 1768 tells of two ladies who incurred the wrath of one planter when they sallied forth in their carriage to solicit a vote for his opponent.[15] The letters of the governors also make it clear that they used their considerable influence at one time or another to secure the election of members friendly to their administrations, often with great success.

Those elected to the Assembly were supposed to own at least five hundred acres of land, but this requirement had little meaning, for only the most prosperous planters and merchants in this young and relatively poor colony could afford to give up sometimes as much as five or six months of the year for several years to serve without pay in the legislature at Savannah. If it be true that in 1757 there were not ten men in the colony worth five hundred pounds,[16] it is indeed surprising that nineteen could be found both willing and able to make such a sacrifice of time and money.

The royal governor was so integral a part of Georgia's colonial legislature that his contemporaries considered him the first of its three branches. The governor, the Council, or the Assembly could introduce legislation, and all but the governor had the power of amendment. The governor, in practice, only advocated the passage of certain measures or engaged a private member of the Council or Assembly to propose whatever he wished enacted. The Council nearly always introduced at least a few bills in every session, although its right to do so was

14. *Ga. Gaz.*, Oct. 4, 1769; *South-Carolina Gazette; And Country Journal* (Charleston), Mar. 24, 1772.
15. May 4, May 11.
16. Ellis to William Pitt, Aug. 1, 1757, unpub. Col. Records, XXVIII, Part 1, 57-60.

sometimes challenged after 1766; but for the most part it contented itself with amending, approving, or rejecting bills sent up from the lower house. The Assembly initiated most of the legislation. All money bills originated there and could not be amended by the Council. Before any bill was sent to the governor, it had to be approved by both houses. No bill became law until the governor had given his assent. Acts of a general nature were not supposed to become law until reviewed and approved in London.

For the most part, the royal governor was able to carry his point in the legislature through his influence with individual assemblymen, the influence naturally accruing from the power and prestige of his office. But whenever persuasion did not suffice, the governor could resort to political pressures of various sorts. As long as he retained the support of his Council and backing from Britain, which he ordinarily took pains to do, the governor exercised, in effect, a triple veto on the proposals of the Commons House of Assembly. Should he fail to intimidate an aroused House, he could at any time adjourn or dissolve the legislature. In elections following dissolution, the voters of the colony, by returning the governor's enemies to the lower house, sometimes produced a deadlock between the Assembly and the governor. At this juncture the governor had every advantage. The civil establishment of Georgia was supported by funds from Britain and consequently was not dependent upon the appropriations of the local legislature. The governor could, and did on occasion, carry on the business of government, sometimes for years, without ever calling the legislature into session. The Liberty Boys learned just how impregnable the royal governor's constitutional position was when in 1775 they were forced to go outside the established government in order to seize power.

Potentially and in theory the power of the governor was great from the very beginning of royal rule; but had it been absolute it would have meant little while Georgia remained an empty and terror-ridden land. Each governor in turn recognized that the success of his administration and the future of the colony depended upon his ability to attract new settlers. Not until thousands of industrious immigrants had come in could Georgia begin to be either strong or productive. The governors also knew that few were likely to come so long as the government of Georgia could offer no security from Indian attack. Men were not generally disposed to invest their property and their labor in a place where there was little or nothing to hinder the Indians from cutting the throats of their families, their slaves, and their livestock. During the first decade of royal government, the governors devoted their energy and authority to solving the problem of defense. Although John Reynolds did little to remedy the deplorable state of the military establishment in the colony, his successor, Henry Ellis (1757-1760), laid the foundations of the defense structure upon which James Wright (1760-1782) built to contribute to the clear-cut ascendancy of the whites over the Creeks in the next decade. Both Ellis and Wright erected forts and strengthened the militia. Because of their efforts, troops in the pay of the British government were stationed in the colony and kept there until 1767 when the increase in population allowed Georgia to defend herself against sudden attack.

Indispensable as it was, force was not the only instrument of the broad Indian policy adopted by both Ellis and Wright. Their skill in treating with the Indians earned for both a well-deserved reputation for astuteness in Indian affairs. By tact and persuasion and by the manipulation of intertribal rivalries as much as by the threat of punishment, Ellis helped hold the Indians at bay. Wright's sternness, unclouded by wishful thinking and tempered by consistent fairness, served the same purpose. Wright won the initiative from the Indians, never to relinquish it, after the withdrawal of the French and Spanish from the scene in 1763, leaving the Creeks and Cherokee dependent on British goods and at the mercy of British arms. The greater security offered to settlers thereafter encouraged many to come to this frontier; the arrival of every potential militia-man meant a gain in strength for the colony and a relative loss for the Indians. As late as 1773, word that the Creeks were on the warpath was enough to throw the backcountry into a panic; but twenty years of royal rule had given the colony the strength to assure its survival, let the Indians do what they would.

Though preoccupied with defense, the governors did not neglect the task of providing land for newcomers. A bountiful supply of cheap but fertile land was what had brought settlers from Europe to the eastern seaboard of North America in the first place, and it was now drawing them inland to the westward, to the mountains and beyond. Each of the three royal gov-ernors undertook to assure that nothing impeded the rapid conversion of the vast woodlands of Georgia into farms and plantations. If Georgia was to grow and prosper, the governors realized, the vacant land in the colony had to be transferred with maximum dispatch from the king to those of his subjects who would settle on it and cultivate it. The colonial governors and the Board of Trade were in agreement that the land policy for Georgia should be directed solely to populating the colony and making it productive. The prospects of future returns in the form of increased trade made the British government will-ing to forego any attempt to obtain immediate revenue by sell-ing the land. The only disagreement about land policy between the Board and the governors arose from what was really only a difference in emphasis. Entrusted with the task of defending the colony against the Indians, Governor Ellis and Governor Wright wished to limit the size of the holdings so as to use the land to attract as many whites to this frontier as possible; the Board of Trade, primarily concerned with the expansion of commerce, was intent upon putting the land into the hands of those best able to cultivate it. The English officials were in-clined to look with equanimity on a man's holdings, no matter how extensive, so long as he had the capital and slaves to make his plantations productive. With the Board setting the policy and the governor putting it into effect, a compromise between the two points of view naturally evolved.[17]

Governor Reynolds found the whole business of ownership and disposition of public land in a state of confusion when he took office in 1754. The Trustees, who had planted the colony and for nearly twenty years governed it, had been neither consistent nor businesslike in their land policy. The ambiguity and irregularity of land titles which resulted were appalling. Before he left England, Reynolds got explicit instructions for introducing a sensible land system in Georgia. The new procedure for acquiring grants was generally acceptable, but the conditions imposed on the ownership of land brought heated protests from the landholders. To retain possession of the land granted him, a man was supposed to clear and cultivate his holdings at the rate of five acres a year. Literal compliance would have left the owner of one hundred acres of land at the end of twenty years without a piece of lumber or a stick of firewood on his farm. Since most tracts included untillable pine land, a farmer was apparently expected to clear land for no useful purpose. Governor Reynolds supported the colonial legislature in seeking an immediate alteration in his instructions in this particular; and in 1755 the Board, protesting that the regulations had been misunderstood, sent additional instructions to Reynolds which removed all objections on this point.

The procedure and requirements for obtaining grants of public land remained unchanged from 1755 until the eve of the Revolution. On the first Tuesday of every month, called Land Day, the governor met with the Council in their chamber in Savannah to receive petitions for land. Each petitioner presented a statement setting forth the number of persons in his family (which included servants and slaves) for whom he had

17. Ellis to Board of Trade, Mar. 20, May 5, 1757, Apr. 24, 1759, *ibid.*, 16-17, 18-31, 291-303; Wright to Board of Trade, Apr. 20, 1763, *ibid.*, 730-38; Board of Trade to Ellis, Apr. 21, 1758, *ibid.*, XXXIV, 220-36.

received no land from the colony. As the head of a household he was entitled to one hundred acres for himself and fifty acres for each dependent, white or black. If a man was judged capable of cultivating more than the acreage allotted him under this formula, the governor could sell him up to one thousand additional acres at the nominal price of one shilling for every ten acres. In his petition to the governor, the applicant included a general description of the location of the desired tract and a pledge that the land was intended for his own use. After hearing the applicant swear to the truth of the statements in his petition, the governor issued a warrant directing the surveyor general to have the described tract surveyed.

If all went well, a plat certified by the surveyor was returned to the attorney general's office within six months. The attorney general prepared a fiat and forwarded it with the plat to the office of the colonial secretary. The grant was then prepared by the secretary, signed by the governor in Council, countersigned by the clerk of the Council, stamped with the seal by the secretary, and finally recorded by the register. His fees paid, the petitioner held title to the land subject to the condition that he cultivate three out of every fifty plantable acres in his grant.[18]

Although this procedure was certainly simple and liberal enough, Governor Reynolds and Governor Ellis had trouble gaining its full acceptance. Some of the colonists, accustomed to taking the warrant for survey as sufficient to establish ownership, balked at going to the trouble and expense of obtaining new grants in order to clear their titles to land received from the Trustees. By the time Governor Wright took office, however, Georgia had a well-ordered land office which operated efficiently until the public land policy was changed in 1773-74.

18. Reynolds to Board of Trade, Jan. 25, Feb. 28, Oct. 8, 1755, *ibid.*, XXVII, 120-21, 126-29, 182-90; Journal of Upper House, Jan. 22, 1755, *Col. Records*, XVI, 20-23; Reynolds' Instructions and supplementary Instructions, unpub. Col. Records, XXXIV, 24-82, 155-58; John Pownall to Reynolds, June 5, 1755, *ibid.*, 139-44; Wright to Shelburne, May 15, 1767, *ibid.*, XXXVII, 206-12; Wright to Board of Trade, June 8, 1768, *ibid.*, XXVIII, Part 2, 560-77.

Grants for nearly 550,000 acres had been recorded under the supervision of the governors by 1767 without any other public complaint of discrimination than the feeling expressed by some that Governor Reynolds himself had been perhaps a trifle greedy.[19]

To attract the men needed for the colony's development, Governor Wright also undertook to find new land for prospective immigrants. Much of the best available land had been claimed before 1760. At the end of the French and Indian War, Wright got from the Creeks a cession of nearly two and one-half million acres, tripling the size of the colony. The extension of the province south of the Altamaha River after the Spanish withdrawal from Florida added another million or so acres to the land reserve. Finally, in 1773, Wright got permission to assume the large debts owed to white traders by the Creeks and the Cherokee, in return for something like two million acres of choice land at the northwestern extremity of the province. In all, Governor Wright added more than six million acres to the approximately one million inherited from the Trustees by Governor Reynolds.

The successful land and Indian policies of the royal governors opened the floodgates for a flow of settlers which doubled Georgia's population in the first decade of royal rule and then doubled it again in the next. In 1753, only 2,381 white people lived in the colony. Two years later Governor Reynolds counted 4,500. Immigration was brought almost to a standstill at mid-decade by the outbreak of hostilities with France and by Reynolds' inept handling of colonial affairs, but during Governor Ellis's administration the white population increased until it stood at nearly 7,000 in 1760. From the end of the French and Indian War until the Revolution, the population of Georgia increased rapidly. There were 10,000 whites in

19. In January 1759, 304,884 acres had been granted (Journal of Assembly, Jan. 22, 1759, *Col. Records*, XIII, 349). In 1774, "A Friend to Georgia" estimated the acreage granted at two million, in a broadside dated July 25, 1774, bound with the *Georgia Gazette* in the Georgia Historical Society.

1766, and double that ten years later. The slave population more than kept the pace. Between 1753 and 1773 the number of Negroes increased from 1,000 to 15,000. The thirty-five or forty thousand people in Georgia at the outset of the Revolution made up an insignificant part of the American population; but the rapid growth which the numbers represented is significant. And they were only the forerunners of the tens of thousands soon to follow.[20]

The whites who came into Georgia before the Revolution, the majority coming after 1763, were in many respects a motley crew. Much has been said about the cosmopolitan population of colonial Georgia. The refugees from the English debtors' prisons sent out by the Trustees have shared attention with the Salzburgers, the Moravians, the Acadians, the Scottish Highlanders, the Scots from northern Ireland, the Jews, the Quakers, and the occasional continental Europeans, all of whom gave a touch of color to the predominantly Anglo-American population of the colony. It is difficult, however, to discover what influence, if any, these people had on the character or the institutions of Georgia. The Acadians and Moravians came and went before the Revolution, leaving not a trace. The Salzburgers in general kept to themselves, even to clinging to their native tongue, and left the conduct of their outside affairs largely to the care of their able ministers. Few in number, the miscellaneous Europeans and Jews of Savannah made little impact upon the colony. These peoples, many of whom had come to the New World in search of religious freedom, had no desire to meddle with the English civil institutions which gave them the protection they longed for. Besides, scarcely any of them belonged to the influential classes. Those who did, such

20. Ga. Hist. Soc., *Colls.*, III, 158-79; De Brahm, *History of Georgia*, 50; unpub. Col. Records, XXVIII, Part 2, 414-40; Reynolds to Board of Trade, Jan. 5, 1756, *ibid.*, XXVII, 237-43; Ellis to Board of Trade, Jan. 28, 1759, *ibid.*, XXVIII, Part 1, 252-56; Ellis to William Pitt, Aug. 1, 1757, *ibid.*, 57-60; Wright to Board of Trade, Apr. 15, 1761, *ibid.*, 511-16; Wright to Dartmouth, Dec. 27, 1773, Mar. 2, Apr. 26, May 18, 1774, *ibid.*, XXXVIII, Part 1, 158-60, 182-83, 262-64, 275-77.

men as the contentious Joachim Zubly or the Salzburger John Adam Treutlen, seem to have adopted the attitudes of the *nouveau* petty English gentry with whom they associated. The two settlements of Scots also remained outside the main stream of Georgia history during these years. Those who came from northern Ireland in the late sixties and early seventies to settle the upcountry town of Queensborough were poor and without influence; and not until the Revolution, when their military talents won them prominence, did the Highlanders at Darien come into their own.

Georgia was in plain fact English. The business of the colony was conducted by men of British ancestry who were familiar with and devoted to English institutions and English law. Yet it was English only in the colonial or American sense. Georgia was an American colony and a majority of its people in the years before the Revolution were Americans. Many more of the men living in Georgia in 1776 were native born, or born in Carolina and Virginia and in the northern colonies or in the West Indies, than had come out from Britain. Because most of the people who settled in Georgia after 1754 were drawn from other parts of North America, the American character of the colony became more pronounced with each passing year.[21]

The backcountry of Georgia was particularly American in its character and in its antecedents. Even in 1754, the fertile land on the western bank of the Savannah River above the sandy coastal plain had closer ties with the South Carolina upcountry than with the more English Georgia coast. South Carolina upcountrymen had been drifting across the river before Governor Reynolds' arrival, even before Oglethorpe's, often in search of grazing land for their cattle. Until 1763, there was only a scattering of farms back from the river, but with the cession of new lands and the decline of Indian power

---

21. The records of the land court reveal that only rarely did a man from outside the thirteen colonies apply for land in Georgia after 1754.

in this area, the South Carolinians were joined by the up-countrymen of North Carolina and Virginia in emigrating to Georgia by the thousands and, after the Revolution, by the tens of thousands.

Here, in the country about Augusta, the wild and rough frontiersman held sway. In the 1770's decent farmers attracted by the plenitude of good land began to give this section some semblance of permanence and respectability, but the wide expanse of land, unsettled and remote, was a magnet for the lawless, the irresponsible, and the ne'er-do-wells of the Carolina and Virginia upcountry. Gangs of outlaws sprang up in the 1760's to terrorize the people on both sides of the river, murdering and pillaging much as they pleased. Savannah and Charleston were almost as foreign to them as London, and as little to be feared. The gentlemen of the lowcountry, for their part, were inclined to look upon these Crackers as no great improvement on the savage Indians they replaced. The upcountry farms became the cotton plantations of the next century, but the lawless tradition was long in dying. Augusta, the metropolis of the upcountry, remained an eye-gouging, nose-biting, rip-roaring frontier town long after cotton became king.[22]

Important though they were by force of sheer numbers, the American-born upcountrymen were only the chorus in the drama acted out in Georgia in the days of the royal governors. The planters and merchants of the tidewater were the actors. They were the people who counted, economically and politi-

22. An Account of Lands Allotted by the President and Assistants. . . , unpub. Col. Records, XXVII, 192-223; James Habersham to Hillsborough, June 15, Aug. 12, 1772, *ibid.*, XXXVII, 651-53, XXXVIII, Part 1, 4-8; Wright to Board of Trade, Aug. 15, 1767, *ibid.*, XXVIII, Part 2, 517-19; Ellis to Lyttelton, May 1, 1757, Lyttelton Papers, Clements Lib.; Journal of Assembly, Jan. 27, 1763, *Col. Records*, XIV, 9-10; *Pennsylvania Gazette* (Philadelphia), Sept. 10, 1767; *S. C. Gaz.*, July 23, 1768–Apr. 6, 1769; Anthony Stokes, *A View of the Constitution of the British Colonies, in North-America and the West-Indies, at the Time the Civil War Broke Out on the Continent of America* . . . (London, 1783), 140-42. Stokes says of the Crackers: "It is highly probable that these people will in time overrun the rice part of the country, as the Tartars in Asia have done by the fruitful cultivated provinces in the southern parts of that country."

cally. Their plantations and their trading activity were the main sources of Georgia's new-found wealth. As a class they provided the political leadership of the colony: in fact, the merchants and planters, with the governor, who was himself a leading planter, *were* the government. They were the men on whom Ellis and Wright relied to adopt and carry out the policies which were so greatly beneficial to Georgia. Beginning with the Stamp Act troubles, Governor Wright was faced with opposition led by one faction of this merchant-planter class and dependent for support on another faction of the same class. When the break came in 1775, it was a faction of merchants and planters who lost power along with Wright, and it was a faction of merchants and planters who wrested control from Wright. The people in general had a choice, and their choice decided the issue; but they could choose only between government by loyalist gentlemen and government by rebel gentlemen.

The merchant-planter class in Georgia can almost be said to have had its beginning with the arrival of the first royal governor. To be more exact, the legalizing of slavery near the end of the Trustee period was the occasion for the first significant immigration of propertied people into the colony. After 1750 some of the heavily indebted slaveholders in South Carolina were encouraged by their creditors to take their mortgaged slaves into Georgia where good land, almost free for the asking, and low taxes promised quicker returns from their planting than in South Carolina. Among the first of the Carolina planters to come in were Jonathan Bryan, Francis Arthur, James Deveaux, Benjamin Farley, James Maxwell, and the Gibbons brothers, all of whom in a short time became prosperous and influential citizens of the province.[23] By the time Governor

23. De Brahm, *History of Georgia,* 51; Ottolenghé to Benjamin Martin, Nov. 25, 1754, unpub. Col. Records, XXVII, 86-90; Reynolds to Board of Trade, Mar. 29, 1756, *ibid.,* 259-63; Ellis to Board of Trade, May 5, 1757, *ibid.,* XXVIII, Part 1, 18-31; Proceedings and Minutes of the President and Assistants, 1741-1754, *Col. Records,* VI, 333-34, 376, 404, 439, 447; Lilla M. Hawes, ed., "Proceedings of the President and Assistants in Council of Georgia, 1749-

Reynolds took office, the South Carolina Congregationalists had almost completed their removal from Dorchester and Beech Hill to a tract of land reserved for them on the Midway River in Georgia. Arriving with only a few slaves, they extended their holdings so rapidly that by 1760 their plantations were among the largest in the colony and the town of Sunbury on the Midway had become a busy little port.[24] At the close of the French and Indian War the influx of men of property quickened and continued until the Revolution. James Bulloch, father of Archibald, Joseph Tatnall, and John Mullryne were the most substantial of the South Carolina planters who decided to try their fortunes in Georgia in the mid-sixties. Although most of the established planters who came were from South Carolina, there were also men like Leonard Claiborne from Virginia and Clement Martin, Edmund Tannatt, and Lewis Johnson from the West Indies who transferred their planting operations to the new colony.[25]

Not all of Georgia's leaders came from the other American colonies. A few of the early English settlers weathered the lean years under the Trustees and lived on into the royal period to become prominent merchants and planters, notably James Habersham, Francis Harris, and Noble Jones. Sons of these and other early settlers reached manhood before the Revolution and formed an important segment of Georgia's governing class. Britishers with connections in Georgia, Joseph Clay and James Jackson among others, came out from England during Wright's administration; but most important of the late arrivals from England were the royal officials sent by the king. They were a

1751," Part II, *Georgia Historical Quarterly*, XXXVI (Mar. 1952), 69; Ellis to Lyttelton, Apr. 1757, Lyttelton Papers, Clements Lib.

24. Proceedings, 1741-1754, *Col. Records*, VI, 458-59; Minutes of Gov. and Council, *ibid.*, VII, 178; Ellis to Board of Trade, Oct. 22, 1757, unpub. Col. Records, XXVIII, Part 1, 97-101; Wright to Board of Trade, Dec. 23, 1760, Oct. 1, 1762, *ibid.*, 477-88, 647-50.

25. Reynolds to Board of Trade, Sept. 22, 1755, unpub. Col. Records, XXVII, 179-80; Minutes of Gov. and Council, *Col. Records*, IX, 135-36, 284, 366, 382, 482, 506-7, 577, 642; Proceedings, 1741-1754, *ibid.*, VI, 442.

prosperous and powerful group, and, with some of the Scottish merchants who appeared in Savannah as its shipping increased, they composed the hard core of Wright's support, most of them eventually following him into exile after 1775.

The leading planters of Georgia during the royal period were those who cultivated rice and indigo along the coast. Every year rice comprised roughly one third of the value of the colony's exports.[26] As the yield from the rice fields of Georgia climbed from about three thousand barrels in 1754 to nearly fifteen thousand in 1769, the value of the exports from Savannah and Sunbury increased at about the same annual rate. The growth in power and wealth of the individual rice planter was proportionately greater because the increase in rice production was not accompanied by a comparable increase in the number of rice planters. Their number was limited by the supply of land suitable for the growing of rice and by the high initial cost of establishing a rice plantation. Because rice fields were confined to that part of the banks of coastal streams which could be flooded with fresh water at high tide, such land was quick to be claimed. A prospective rice planter arriving in Georgia after 1760 often found that he could not depend upon the grants allowed him by family rights for the type of land which he required. A 200-acre tract containing 130 acres of rice lands could be bought for approximately £200. To cultivate this acreage, the planter needed forty working hands, representing an investment of another £1800. All told, the man wishing to establish a rice plantation of 130 acres had to have at his disposal what amounted to nearly £2500 in capital or credit. In his assertion that during the time of the royal governors "every man that had industry, became opulent,"[27] Chief Justice Stokes overlooked the enormous advantage enjoyed by

26. This discussion of the cultivation and marketing of rice is drawn largely from the following sources: *Letters of Habersham, 1756-1775,* Ga. Hist. Soc., *Colls.,* VI; *Ga. Gaz.,* 1763-69; De Brahm, *History of Georgia;* Wright's Answers, 1773, unpub. Col. Records, XXVIII, Part 2, 414-40; Wright's "Report," 1773, in Ga. Hist. Soc., *Colls.,* III, 158-79.
27. Stokes, *A View of the Constitution of the British Colonies,* 139.

the prospective planter who came into Georgia with a few slaves and access to capital. The planters of South Carolina who became rice planters in colonial Georgia did so not only because they were experienced in the culture of rice but because their previous venture left some with the means to convert the Georgia swamplands into rice fields.

Anyone able to make a start as a rice planter in Georgia before the Revolution, with luck, became in a few years a man of wealth and power in the province. Under favorable circumstances a planter cultivating 130 acres of rice with forty slaves could expect to harvest 350 barrels of rice. This he could normally sell for about £700, a gross return of 25 to 30 per cent on his initial investment. Although very few men arrived in Georgia with as many as forty slaves, the high profit on rice, the low cost of its cultivation with slave labor, and easy credit enabled a planter to expand his planting interests rapidly once a start had been made. For instance, the administrators of the estate of a planter named Farley increased (with some help from the Negroes themselves) the twenty-six slaves on the plantation to fifty-five in the five years from 1765 to 1770.[28]

Even after he had acquired the land and slaves to begin his plantation, the successful planter had to have the skill to master the intricacies of rice cultivation and the good fortune to escape the many hazards attached to it. He first had to fix the banks of the streams which ran through his land so he could control the flow of the tide into his cleared fields. In the spring his Negro hands planted the rice seedlings in the flooded fields and watered the plants with the tide until it was time to let the rice ripen in the sun. A prolonged drought in the early summer could cut the yield to a small fraction of what was hoped for. A storm flooding a field of ripened rice might destroy the crop. Barring some disaster, the planter had his slaves harvest and thresh the rice in the fall. Then he stored it in his barn or took it immediately to market in Savannah or Sunbury.

28. Gibbons Papers, Duke.

The first barrels of new rice each year came into Savannah late in the fall, how late depending on the season; but the greater part of the crop was brought into town after Christmas, when the planter exchanged rice and indigo for the goods which the Savannah merchant had imported from abroad, mostly from Britain. Besides the essential supplies for his plantation, he bought English cloth to be made into breeches and coats for himself and his sons, finery of all sorts for his womenfolk, and enough rough material to give his slaves their annual change of clothing. English furniture and plate for his home, carriages, fine wines and West Indian rum, and other luxuries also tempted him. But the bulk of his harvest went to repay the merchant who had advanced him the credit to finance his crop. With the credit, he had bought the slaves and supplies used to cultivate new rice fields during the past season; by his prompt remittance, he was likely to obtain new credit with which he could again expand his planting in the next season. For the planter who was striving to build up his holdings, as most were, the great object was not to clear himself of debt but to get additional credit every year for further expansion. The result was that a planter's indebtedness tended to increase rather than to decrease as his planting operations became larger.

The expansion of rice culture in Georgia after 1760 gave rise to the foreign trade which centered around the port of Savannah. The planter was father to the merchant, and his crops were the merchant's *raison d'être*. Until slaves were brought into the colony and employed in the rice fields, the export-import trade of Georgia was practically nonexistent. Before 1760, the company of Harris and Habersham was the only established firm at Savannah engaged in the overseas trade. The South Carolina merchants handled much of the inconsequential trade between Georgia and Britain through the port of Charleston. Savannah merchants like Thomas Rasberry were little more than the Georgia agents for Charleston mercantile firms; but, as the production of the plantations in Georgia increased in the 1760's, commerce of a different sort began to be carried on at Savannah. Savannah became a port in its own right, independent of Charleston; and its merchants were soon conducting complex and large-scale trading operations throughout the British Empire.

Of prime importance to the coastal merchant reaching out for a share of Georgia's growing overseas trade in the 1760's and 1770's was the establishment of a working agreement with one or more merchants in Britain to look after his affairs on that side of the water. The arrangements varied in detail, but a British merchant connected with the Georgia trade was ordinarily obliged to find a market in Britain for the produce shipped over by his Georgia associate and to supply him with British goods for the colonial market. Similar but less profitable arrangements were made on generally a much smaller scale by the Savannah or Sunbury merchants with business houses in Charleston or Philadelphia. The Georgia merchants also carried on some foreign trade at Savannah itself. Occasionally an independent ship captain arrived with a cargo of goods which he used to bargain for rice and other produce on the local market. Guinea traders made their way up the river with shiploads of Negroes for sale. West Indian sugar, molasses, rum, and slaves were brought in and sold for the lumber and foodstuffs needed in the islands.

As extensive as it became, the trade radiating out from Savannah by no means monopolized the attention of the larger firms of the town. In the off-season the owner of a seagoing vessel at Savannah sometimes found himself engaged in trade between two foreign ports. And the search for profitable foreign outlets for local produce was only one aspect of the Savannah merchant's trading activities. He also provided the colony with goods and supplies imported from abroad. His best customer was the lowcountry planter. Since most business in the colony was done on credit and often virtually by barter, a planter customarily attached himself more or less permanently and exclusively to a particular merchant who supplied him with what he needed and at harvest time took over his crop in payment on his account. The large Savannah commercial houses also furnished the smaller merchants throughout the colony with goods for their stores. Being neither importers nor exporters, these lesser merchants turned over to the company at Savannah the rice and indigo collected from their customers. The traders in the Indian country also got their supplies from the Savannah merchant. They sent down the river from Augusta the deer and beaver skins which were important items in the coastal merchant's shipments to Britain.

Diverse though it was, both within the colony and throughout the Empire, the commercial activity of Georgia after 1763 rested mainly on the relations of the Savannah and Sunbury merchants with the lowcountry planters on the one hand and with the British merchants on the other. The heart of the colony's trade was the exchange of the produce raised on the plantations for goods manufactured in England. Rice from the plantations was the staple of the British purchases from Georgia, and manufactured articles from Britain probably accounted for 60 to 70 per cent of the imports into Georgia every year.

The difficulties and risks involved in getting rice from the Georgia planter to the British merchant were great. Careful and shrewd calculations were necessary at every step. First, the colonial merchant had to arrange with the local planters for the rice. To secure the desired amount, he often had to contract for the crop before it was made. His offer to the planter was of necessity based on an estimate of prices current several months later, the accuracy of which depended in great measure on the quality of the rice and on how early it was brought to town, neither one a matter of certainty in August or even September. Once he had the rice stored in his warehouse on the river, the merchant's next task was to get it to England safely and with dispatch. Months of planning were necessary if the needed shipping was to be in the river at the proper time. After the merchant had supervised the loading of the ship and secured its clearance, he insured his cargo and prayed for a safe and speedy landfall in Britain. Speed was important throughout the entire operation, for the first shipments of rice to get to British ports each season usually brought premium prices. Even when the ship's captain had delivered his cargo to the British factor, the Savannah merchant's worries were not over. Unless his associate in Britain was diligent and trustworthy, he might not get the best price for the grain. What was worse, if the Britisher showed poor judgment in purchasing supplies for his Georgia connections and sent out overpriced goods or goods unsuitable for the Georgia market, the colonial merchant might have the distressing experience of seeing his profits dwindle away as unsold goods rotted in his warehouse.

Both merchant and planter in the colony relied on a system of credits to finance expanding operations. The merchants of Savannah largely financed the extension of rice culture by advancing credit to the planters for slaves and supplies. Because the merchant could not make his remittances to his British associate until the planter brought in his crop, he in turn relied on the British merchant to send out goods on credit. The advances from Britain always exceeded the remittances of the colony; which is to say, Georgia's development, agricultural as well as commercial, was financed by British merchants.

The measure of Georgia's dependence upon British credit is to be found in its unbalanced trade with Britain throughout the colonial period. In 1760, the colonists in Georgia bought from abroad nearly three times as much as they shipped. Five years later, the value of the colony's exports, though five times greater than in 1760, still fell short of its imports by nearly £50,000, a difference only partially repaired by various subsidies paid in Georgia by the British government. Increased production narrowed the gap between exports and imports in the last years of Wright's administration but never closed it.

The truth is, the system of credit advances and credit restrictions built up by the British merchants made possible the growth and progress of Georgia in the 1760's and 1770's. The growing indebtedness of Georgia to the British merchants caused no undue alarm as long as the trade and the production of the colony continued to expand—and expand it did. Bare statistics, which reveal an average annual increase in exports of £10,000 during the 1760's, attest to this; but more eloquent and just as convincing are the remarks on the colony's flourishing condition made by the inhabitants in letter after letter, as if they found the true picture of the prosperity of Georgia difficult to convey, and even difficult to believe. The planter contracted new debts every year, but each year he cultivated more rice fields, he owned more slaves, and he made bigger crops. The Savannah merchant gave and received a greater amount of credit each year, but every year his profits increased as he shipped more produce and sold more goods. By sending to Georgia more goods than the produce of the colony could pay for, the British merchant was continually adding to his investment in Georgia. His investment was a profitable one. The market for his goods was constantly growing, and the remittances from the colonial merchant were constantly increasing. Not until 1775, when Britain and the American colonies had placed restrictions on trade which ended this upward spiral, was there such talk as that of the British associate of the Savannah merchant, Edward Telfair, who suggested that the time had come for the merchants and planters in Georgia to abandon the profitable but costly expansion of trade and planting and begin to look to the payment of their debts.

Since credit was easy and the free flow of capital from Britain continued, the new local magnates had little to complain of; but they did share the common colonial dissatisfaction with the restrictions placed upon the issue of paper currency, restrictions imposed by the British government in response to the demands of the English and Scottish merchants that their

American investments be protected against any move on the part of their colonial creditors to inflate the local currency. It was only over the protest of the Board of Trade that Georgia succeeded in issuing somewhat less than £8000 in paper before the passage of the Currency Act of 1764. The subsequent short supply of currency, resulting from the expansion of the economy, was aggravated by the unbalanced trade which drained off the specie that did find its way into Georgia. The shortage of currency, however, remained little more than a serious inconvenience as long as virtually unlimited credit was available.

Most of Georgia's increase in wealth in the decade before the Revolution went to swell the private fortunes of the coastal merchants and the lowcountry planters. They were few in number. In any year probably less than a score of merchants —some themselves engaged in planting—monopolized the export-import trade. The planters who produced most of the rice and indigo for the British trade, and who also owned a fair share of the backcountry land which provided the lumber products and livestock shipped from Georgia to the West Indies, were only a little more numerous. These two groups skimmed off a disproportionate part of the profits arising from the production and sale of colonial produce. Their total number, merchant and planter, was certainly never more than one hundred, and it was probably less than fifty most of the time.

These few men were culled from the generality of settlers by the harsh demands of success on the frontier. They were the men of ambition with the energy and the intelligence (and the luck) to wrest their fortunes from the swamps and virgin woodlands of colonial Georgia. The benevolence of English rule and the wealth of natural resources unclaimed and undeveloped gave individual initiative a free hand. Neither lack of opportunity nor the restrictions of government held a man of ability back. It was the gifted and tough few who became the Savannah merchants and the coastal rice planters of eighteenth-century Georgia, and who together formed a class which dominated the economy of the colony.

The leadership of the merchant-planter class went beyond economic domination. In this small and unformed country the rising merchant or planter soon learned that his private interests were touched by every conceivable aspect of public policy. Every measure of the government dealing with defense, Indians, public land, trade, taxation, currency, crop subsidies, slavery, and the building and maintenance of roads, bridges and ferries, was likely to have an immediate and sometimes vital effect on his planting and trading interests. The prudent man put himself in a position to exercise some control over the decisions made about these things. A seat in the Commons House of Assembly offered to the colonial a position from which he could influence public policy. As members of the Assembly, or less often of the Council, the merchants and planters asserted political as well as economic leadership, though political power had to be shared with the royal governor.

The merchant-planter class and the royal governors emerge as the two protagonists in the story of Georgia during the twenty years before the Revolution. The story is most dramatic at the points of conflict; more often it is a tale of cooperation. In every project which promised to promote the prosperity and security of Georgia the interests of both the Empire and the colony not only allowed but demanded that the two work together. The governors were always more than willing to cooperate with the merchants and planters of the Assembly in their efforts to mold the government into an instrument for subduing this new land and enriching its inhabitants. A flourishing and well-ordered community was exactly what the governors' masters in England desired. The way in which the governors and the colonial leaders combined forces to impose the English pattern on an American frontier is one of the things which make the story worth the telling.

This political alliance for the exploitation of the colony does much to explain the nature and the rapidity of Georgia's development from 1763 to 1775, but the alliance held only so long as the interests of the Empire and the interests of Georgia coincided. As imperial policy after 1763 diverged increasingly from what many of the colonists conceived to be their best interests, a breach between the colonial magnates and the king's representative in Georgia appeared and widened until at length it resolved itself into a struggle for power between Governor Wright and the leaders of the Assembly, a contest which had many implications and raised political questions of the most fundamental sort. This was the time when the future nature of the Empire and the fate of the colonies were being settled. Revolution was moving upon America. Georgia shared in the drama, but belatedly and reluctantly. In relation to the other colonies Georgia was still in the early eighteenth century. As Britain forced the rest of America to the brink of revolution, British policy had a distinctly different effect on Georgia, and Georgia reacted differently to it. This is also part of the story.

James Wright's province did not loom large in the affairs of the British Empire or of America in the years before the Revolution. In all things, Georgia, the youngest of the colonies, small and weak, followed in the wake of her older sisters. Whatever was said or done by the Georgia patriots in opposing Governor Wright was usually said and done sooner and better in every colony to the northward, from Carolina to Massachusetts. And its infant economy, though lusty and growing, was still only an infinitesimal part of the imperial economic system. Yet there is something to be got from a study of Georgia besides special knowledge of local history. To observe the interaction of European man and the American frontier is always instructive; an understanding of the American Revolution and of political revolution in general is enhanced by a close investigation of the quarrel between royal governor and colonists.

For both these things, however, the study of other colonies would serve as well, or better.   But Georgia's story has its peculiar advantage.   Its history in these twenty years serves as something of a summary of a century of colonial development. Coming on the scene late, Georgia after 1754 began to catch up at a rapid rate.   What had engrossed older colonies for years Georgia encompassed in a few months, then passed on to the next level of development.   The history of colonial Georgia, though perhaps as complex as any other, has the merit of brevity.

CHAPTER II

Governor John Reynolds,
1754-1757

THE KING'S GOVERNOR was received by the colony with all the good will in the world. After twenty years of crippling restrictions and inadequate support under the Trustees, the people of Georgia hailed him as the herald of a new day. When John Reynolds came up to the town in his barge on a Tuesday in late October 1754, Savannah gave itself over to a celebration only rivaled by the demonstrations of joy at his departure two and one-half years later. The clanging of bells and the sound of guns firing filled the air, on into the night. Bonfires sprang up after dark and lighted up the town. The "lower Class of People," having no wood for their fires and being "unwilling to lose their Share of Rejoicing," made "a Bonfire of the Guard House, and had nigh done the same with the old Council-House" before several of the more respectable citizens stopped the fun.[1] Although Reynolds was certainly correct in assuming that his government was received with real pleasure by nearly everyone in the colony, such a pitch of enthusiasm could not, of course, be long sustained.[2]

The new Governor had not been in Savannah a week when something happened which was symbolic of things present and an omen of things to come. It was early November. Savannah after twenty years was still a little settlement of cottages set upon the river bluff. One hundred and fifty houses, all

1. *S. C. Gaz.*, Oct. 31, Nov. 7, 1754.
2. Reynolds to Board of Trade, Dec. 5, 1754, unpub. Col. Records, XXVII, 69-72.

wooden, mostly small, and many sagging and rotted, huddled together there; the pine forest stretched behind, seemingly without end, and below lay the salt marshes which crept in from the sea. In the largest of the houses, the old Council House, Governor Reynolds and the councilors were sitting about, ready to take up the business of the day. Someone called attention to the "ruinous Condition" of their meeting place and noted that apparently it was "in great Danger of falling." Hardly had the gentlemen begun to speak of erecting a proper government house when the building fell with a roar about their ears.[3]

The colony, like Savannah, was in a state of premature decay. The introduction of slaves four years before had seemed to bring some life to the struggling little settlements; but Georgia, with less than five thousand inhabitants, all but a few desperately poor, was still in a most precarious condition. Wise leadership was sorely needed. But Captain John Reynolds of His Majesty's Navy was not the man to supply it. Two years and four months after his arrival he left the colony in worse condition than he had found it—his political career buried under the ruins of his failure in Georgia.

The situation which Governor Reynolds faced was by no means an easy one to cope with or even to comprehend. The difficulties were many and diverse. Some were peculiar to Georgia and could be met only by the efforts of the colony itself; others hung to the tail of power politics in Europe and were lashed about as great empires maneuvered for advantage and fought for supremacy across the sea. Yet, despite their diversity, the problems pressing in upon Reynolds were closely related one to another, each dependent on the other for solution and all inextricably bound into one complex whole.

Governor Reynolds realized from the start the absolute necessity of taking steps to assure the survival of the colony against the powerful forces which menaced it from three sides.

3. Minutes of Gov. and Council, Nov. 4, 1754, *Col. Records*, VII, 21; Reynolds to Board of Trade, Dec. 5, 1754, unpub. Col. Records, XXVII, 69-72.

On this all else depended. True, by clinging to the river, beyond which lay Carolina, and to the ocean, where the British fleet ruled, the colony gained in strength; but inland, in every direction, there were Indians who seeing only the weakness of the settlements before them might at any moment turn upon the colonists and destroy them.

To the south, the Spaniards at St. Augustine were cause for concern. Until 1763, when the Spanish gave up Florida, the governor of Georgia could not be entirely certain exactly where his authority ended and where the Spanish governor's began, whether at the Altamaha, the St. Marys, or even at the St. Johns River. Nor did it make matters simpler for him that the little detachment of British troops south of the Altamaha River was under the direction of the governor of South Carolina instead of his own. From the west the long arm of the French Empire reached out of Mobile and New Orleans through the Indian tribes in the French interest. Between the French country and the English settlements along the coast the towns of the Lower Creeks were dotted about, while a kindred nation, the more numerous Upper Creeks, claimed the lands above, to the west of the Savannah River. And to the north of Fort Augusta, in the hills and mountains, the intelligent Cherokee made their home.[4]

Viewing this ominous array of strength from the tidewater or river banks in the lowlands, the individual settler, anxious for his own safety, wished for strong colonial defenses. The governor, as an official of the British Empire, had additional incentive for attempting to keep the threatening forces at bay. Georgia's importance to the imperial system had always been chiefly military. It was created to provide a buffer between the Carolina settlements and the Indians. And this it long continued to be. What financial support Georgia got from Britain

4. The best description of the disposition and strength of the Indians as seen from Savannah at this time was written by Governor James Wright: unpub. Col. Records, XXVIII, Part 2, 414-40.

in the years immediately after it became a royal colony arose in large part from the fact that the French and Spanish had outposts nearby with Indian warriors conveniently at hand for the harassment of the Carolina settlements.

The role of Georgia rapidly assumed new importance after the arrival of the royal governor. Governor Reynolds took over at the moment when clashes between the British colonists and the French in the Ohio Valley were setting off the final, climactic struggle between Britain and France for control of North America. It immediately became the primary task of the Georgia governor to help keep intact Britain's southern frontier in America, and so it remained until 1763. But before Georgia could become a substantial buffer for Carolina, forts had to be built, soldiers trained and stationed at strategic points, a reliable militia organized and held in readiness, and guns and ammunition supplied both to militiamen and to regulars. The colony had neither the men nor the means to support any such establishment. Strong local defense was impossible until new settlers had been brought in and trade and farming vastly extended. But settlers, particularly men with the capital and slaves needed to develop the country, could hardly be expected to cast their lot with Georgia as long as its government could give no assurance that their lives and property would be reasonably secure. The unhappy circle was complete.

Reynolds, quick to perceive the nature of the dilemma, seized upon the handiest solution: the King must ship troops and supplies to Georgia. Letter after letter went home, stressing the deplorable state of the defense establishment and the pressing need for support. Whitehall was busy with other and greater things than the plight of the Governor and his little colony. Britain was girding herself for the coming struggle with the French; men and supplies could ill be spared for this remote frontier. For the most part, the vexing problem was left to the Governor and to his people. Reynolds was on his own.

Before he could deal with the problem of strengthening the colony, Governor Reynolds had to set up the machinery of royal government. The political system which he installed had been slowly evolving in the other British colonies for more than a century and a half. By 1754 colonial government in America was mature and well defined. Reynolds' Instructions described this system in specific and rather detailed terms. Based on long experience, the Instructions anticipated many of the difficulties Reynolds later encountered, particularly in his relations with the lower house of the newly authorized legislature.[5] Fortunately the Governor was dealing with men who understood and accepted this sort of government. Whether in Britain, in the colonies up the coast, or in Georgia, most of the men of the colony had spent their lives under British rule and were accustomed to English law and to English institutions.

Governor Reynolds had no great difficulty in initiating royal government in Georgia; where he failed was in making it an effective instrument for attacking the problems of the colony. He was a poor politician. The powers assigned him certainly gave him the means for making himself the mainspring of government in the colony. Not only did he have the extensive powers exercised by the royal governors of the older colonies, but he had the additional advantage that his salary and the salaries of all crown officials were paid by the King and not by the local Assembly. Yet Reynolds was never able really to establish his authority, which alone could give the system motion and direction, or to hold the support and wholehearted cooperation of the more substantial men of the colony, without which the system could not function smoothly or to good purpose.

The first challenge to Reynolds came from far up the Savannah, from a man who perhaps shared in the general delight at the Governor's arrival, but for reasons of his own. His name was Edmund Gray (Grey). A strange and fasci-

5. *Ibid.*, XXXIV, 24-82.

nating creature, he remains a shadowy but ubiquitous figure in the story of these times. Coming from Virginia to Fort Augusta in 1750, Gray soon began, it was charged, to parcel out land from the public domain to his Virginia friends and to do it, characteristically enough, without always consulting the government down the river at Savannah. He displayed first and last a distinct taste and talent for controversy even though he was a Quaker. In a short time he had set himself up as leader of the opposition to the interim provincial administration. Many of the malcontents and wishful thinkers of the colony turned to him, and by 1754 he was a force to be reckoned with.[6]

Gray saw in Governor Reynolds' appearance, in the change of government, a chance to give his ambition and his peculiar talents free play. Exactly what he dreamed of, what grandiose schemes lay in his mind, is uncertain. Perhaps Gray himself never defined the limits of his ambition. His political enemies spoke and acted as if he intended nothing less than the overthrow of the new royal government; but Gray's character and his subsequent career suggest rather that here was a political adventurer embarking upon a fishing expedition in muddy waters, out for any big fish that might be lurking there.

At any rate, Gray was political realist enough to recognize that he would not go far unless he secured control of the House of Assembly. Consequently he set out to obtain seats for himself and his followers in the first Georgia legislature, which was to meet early in 1755. Gifted with a tongue that stirred men's imaginations, and being himself a curious blend of the radical dreamer and the unscrupulous adventurer, he was able to appeal at once to the people's love of liberty and to their greed, to their hunger for wealth and power. Arousing fear among the freeholders that the coming of royal government threatened

6. Reynolds to Board of Trade, Feb. 28, 1755, *ibid.*, XXVII, 126-29; Lilla M. Hawes, ed., "Proceedings of the President and Assistants in Council of Georgia, 1749-1751," Part I, *Ga. Hist. Quar.*, XXXV (Dec. 1951), 333; Alex M. Hitz, "The Wrightsborough Quaker Town and Township in Georgia," *Bulletin of Friends Historical Association*, XLVI (1957), 10-22.

their liberties, he injected into the campaign a note of tension and bitterness that remained typical of politics until after Reynolds' removal.   He also played upon the cupidity of the frontiersmen by passing around a letter purportedly from a "person of a Noble Family" in England, letting it be known that he and this exalted personage had several interesting schemes afoot, among which was a plan for monopolizing the Indian trade.   Needless to say, only those who supported Gray at the polls could expect preferential treatment when he had reached a position to dispense favors.[7]

Greatest interest in this first Assembly election in Georgia centered on the race in Savannah where four of the nineteen seats were at stake.   Charles Watson, a lawyer of sorts and a former public official, described by one of the opposing candidates as Gray's "Brother in Iniquity & sedition, of equal Fortune, equal Modesty & Sincerity," was the leading candidate of the Gray faction there.   Samuel Marcer (Mercer), expelled from the Board of Assistants in 1750, William Francis, a former official and a militia officer, and a planter named Gibbons, recently come from South Carolina, were the other town candidates supported by Gray.[8]

The voters went to the polls in Savannah on November 30. Gray's lieutenant, Charles Watson, won his seat but the other three candidates favored by Gray did not.   William Francis and Samuel Marcer lost out to Edmund Tannatt, who was destined to be a leader in the Assembly until his death in 1763, and to Joseph Ottolenghé, an obstinate little convert from Judaism who supervised the culture of silk.   Gray himself won his seat from Augusta.

When the new House of Assembly met at Savannah on January 7, 1755, Gray's opponents, encouraged by the outcome of the election, were confident that they could keep him and his

---

7. Reynolds to Board of Trade, Feb. 28, 1755, unpub. Col. Records, XXVII, 126-29; Ottolenghé to Benjamin Martin, Nov. 25, 30, 1754, *ibid.*, 86-90.
8. Ottolenghé to Martin, Nov. 25, 30, 1754, *ibid.*, 86-90.

"restless Children within proper Bounds";[9] but on the third day of the session Gray made a move to challenge the victorious faction. Rising, he read a petition from the defeated candidates, Marcer and Francis, asking that the election of Tannatt and Ottolenghé be set aside because of the "illicit and partial Practises of the returning Officer" at Savannah.[10] There followed ten days of intense political activity from which the new royal governor emerged with his position apparently greatly strengthened.

For two daily sessions, Friday and Monday, the Assembly carried on its business in an atmosphere of deceptive calm. On Friday, January 10, when an attempt to force a vote on the Marcer-Francis petition failed, the House adjourned until Monday. Monday morning it voted unanimously to disqualify on a technicality two members not involved in the controversy—a foolish move as the majority were soon to learn. Then in the afternoon, the committee of privileges and elections invited Marcer and Francis to testify. After hearing the defeated candidates' testimony, the committee voted to recommend to the House the rejection of the petition and the confirmation of the election of the anti-Gray men, Ottolenghé and Tannatt.

The House was not in session on Tuesday but the members returned Wednesday morning to discover that seven of their number were missing, which, added to the two disqualified Monday, left only ten, a bare majority of the House. When the absent members led by Gray and Watson were sent for and promptly sent back word that they had no intention of attending, the remaining assemblymen, certain that Gray's aim was to force new elections, resolved that ten constituted a House and then continued its session.[11]

9. *Ibid.*
10. Journal of Assembly, Jan. 15, 9, 1775, *Col. Records*, XIII, 24-25, 18.
11. Journal of Assembly, Jan. 10-15, 1755, *ibid.*, 19-27. The House immediately adopted the committee's recommendation that the Marcer-Francis petition be rejected, and then it disqualified two other absent members, which meant that there were four disqualified and five absent. However, the four

In the meantime the seceding members had not been idle. On the same day, January 15, they addressed a circular letter to the freeholders calling for all who "regard the liberties of your Country" to come immediately to Savannah.[12] Although the authors of the letter later insisted that its only purpose was to bring the voters of the vicinity into town to lend by their presence support to Marcer and Francis in their claim to seats in the Assembly,[13] the administration forces were alarmed. But this was just the sort of situation that the old naval officer Reynolds knew how to handle. Catching wind of Gray's activities, he called a meeting of his Council on Friday, January 17, where he was told of the letter urging the citizenry to descend upon Savannah. He immediately issued a proclamation forbidding "all tumultuous Assemblies and nightly Meetings" and instructing all good subjects to prepare to defend the government if the need arose.[14] On the morning of the twentieth Reynolds again met with his Council and read them the letter (luckily "intercepted in the Country") which the seceding assemblymen had addressed to the freeholders.[15] Exaggerating the danger, the Council and the House of Assembly, with other friends of the administration, formed an armed association, and the Governor sent to Charleston for a sloop of war.[16]

Now ready to meet the challenge head-on, the Assembly sent for Edmund Gray on the twenty-first only to discover that he had "gone up the River" and that his compatriots had fled town.[17] On January 27, Gray and Watson along with the

disqualified members joined with Gray and three of the other four absent ones in the attack on the attenuated Assembly. (James Deveaux refused to go along and later claimed that he was forced by the Gray men to absent himself.)
12. Journal of Assembly, Jan. 20, 1755, *ibid.*, 33-34; Minutes of Gov. and Council, Jan. 20, 1755, *ibid.*, VII, 97.
13. Journal of Assembly, Feb. 26, 1755, *ibid.*, XIII, 68.
14. Minutes of Gov. and Council, Jan. 17, 1755, *ibid.*, VII, 94-95.
15. Minutes of Gov. and Council, Jan. 20, 1755, *ibid.*, 96.
16. Minutes of Gov. and Council, Sept. 12, 1755, *ibid.*, 252; S. C. Gaz., Feb. 6, 1755.
17. Journal of Assembly, *Col. Records*, XIII, 35.

other members who had signed the "seditious" letter were expelled by the Assembly.[18] Taking the position that if he could not have all he would have none, Gray with his Virginia friends headed south and crossed over the Altamaha, where no government could reach him.[19] Had he been less impatient, less greedy for power, Gray could undoubtedly have had a commanding voice in colonial affairs. As the acknowledged spokesman of a strong faction in the little Assembly, he would have loomed large there and, in fact, might well have joined forces a year later with Reynolds and his lieutenant, William Little, to put to rout the same faction that had for the moment thwarted him. But this was not Gray's style, and when the Governor adjourned the General Assembly on March 7, 1755, Reynolds and his supporters in the legislature were in complete control.

Here in the spring of 1755 everything favored the Royal Governor's taking a strong and effective lead in colonial affairs. The need for this was obvious enough; the colony was, and had been for years, in a deplorable condition. And the power to act was his; the members of the Council and the leaders of the Assembly, drawn into close alliance with the Governor by the Gray affair, were ready and eager to follow his lead, to co-operate with him in any measures to strengthen the position of the colony. But this was not to be. Reynolds failed to come forward with any proposals for attacking the problems of the colony, and he failed to appreciate and make use of the strong backing of the most substantial men of the country that the rout of the Gray forces had given him. Instead he promptly, almost systematically, alienated these people in both houses of the legislature, eventually inducing a sort of political paralysis. It is a sorry story and perhaps hardly worth the telling: the tale of a man in office frittering away his political assets, reckless both of the welfare of his charge and of his own reputation—

18. *Ibid.*, 38-39.
19. Reynolds to Board of Trade, Apr. 7, 1755, unpub. Col. Records, XXVII, 143-44.

a tale of political stupidity. But in some ways it is instructive. Reynolds' incapacity for constructive political action made the talents of his successors shine the brighter, not only in retrospect but in the eyes of contemporaries. This, indeed, helps to explain the extraordinary success of Ellis and Wright in getting and holding the support of the colonists. And although most of Reynolds' record is negative, the record of failure, it reveals much about the workings of colonial government and politics and about the seasoning of the colonial politician in Georgia.

The assemblymen had hardly left town before trouble developed between the Governor and the members of his Council. The ingredients for conflict lay close at hand. Patrick Graham, James Habersham, and Noble Jones, the senior councilors, had long taken a leading part in the government of the colony. Immediately before Reynolds' appointment they had actually governed the province. Firm but tactful handling was clearly called for. Instead Reynolds treated these men in a way that could not have humiliated and enraged them more had that been his purpose. His instructions placed on many of his powers the proviso that he obtain "the advice and consent" of the Council; he took this to mean that the Council should automatically put their stamp of approval on anything he should do or propose. Any disagreement with him or criticism of his proposals was a personal affront. The arguments and endless discussions of Council meetings understandably were exasperating in the extreme to such a man. On one occasion he burst out with a rude statement fairly bristling with irritation which began as if he were reading an order of the day to a fractious ship's company: "I expect that no Member of this Board will presume again to tell me in Council. . . ."[20]

Reynolds' great complaint was that the councilors, who "would fain have all things Determined by Vote,"[21] acted as if the governor had "no Power to determine in anything, with-

20. Minutes of Gov. and Council, *Col. Records*, VII, 267.
21. Reynolds to Board of Trade, Mar. 29, 1756, unpub. Col. Records, XXVII, 259-63.

out their concurrence."[22] He could have done much to remove this particular bone of contention had he honestly wished to give the Council its fair share of power, by simply informing it of its rights; but, as one councilor put it, "he dont communicate to them his Majesty's Instructions relative to their Duty, otherwise than by Reading these himself in an unintelligible manner."[23] The result was that the Council, jealous of its rights and suspicious of the Governor, not being certain exactly when it should be consulted, did demand a voice at times when the governor was authorized to act alone, to the intense annoyance of Reynolds.

By the summer of 1755 Reynolds was more and more ignoring the Council and relying instead upon his private secretary, William Little, for advice and support. Little, a naval surgeon and a shipmate of Reynolds for twenty years, had come to Georgia with the Governor. With shocking extravagance of his patronage (if nothing more), Governor Reynolds had given Little seven of the offices which he was empowered to fill, including that of clerk of the general court, clerk of the House of Assembly, and commissioner of Indian affairs. The accusation of one councilor that "the Inability of Mr. Reynolds, the Governor of Georgia, conferd, in a few months after his arrival there, the whole Administration of Affairs on Wm Little" could be dismissed as no more than evidence of the natural jealousy and suspicion usually felt for the king's favorite, if the record did not show that this was just about what happened.[24]

In the first stormy session of the General Assembly, Little had been a familiar figure in both houses of the legislature, speaking to members in the name of the Governor "chiefly," he said, "about such Things as could not with any Propriety be

22. Reynolds to Board of Trade, Sept. 22, 1755, *ibid.*, 179-80.
23. Memorial of Alexander Kellett, July 7, 1756, *ibid.*, 273-79.
24. *Ibid.;* Reynolds' Answer to a "State of Facts," *ibid.*, XXVIII, Part 1, 187-213; Representations of Commissioners of Trade and Plantations concerning Gov. Reynolds, July 29, 1756, *ibid.*, XXXIV, 171-95; Minutes of Gov. and Council, *Col. Records*, VII, 251-62.

committed to writing,"[25] and often, it was charged, without the Governor's knowledge.[26] Before the end of the session, Mr. Little had become so sure of his power that he had felt at liberty to withhold from the Governor a bill passed by both houses simply because of what he himself considered "it's Insignificancy and Non-Importance."[27] Whether it was with the design of ultimately creating a faction in the Assembly loyal to himself, which was the actual outcome, or whether to conciliate the enemies of royal government, as he maintained, it is a fact that Little had refused to join the association formed to protect the government against Gray's crowd and that he went to great lengths to cultivate the expelled and disqualified members of the Assembly during and after the session of the legislature. This coupled with the coolness, then rudeness and scorn, shown the Council by the Governor's favorite made it plain that Reynolds was fast abandoning his natural political allies, the appointed Council whose members were the leading men of the community and holders of most of the important offices.

In September 1755 the Council addressed to Reynolds a memorial containing a number of serious charges against Little.[28] In the light of these disclosures, the councilors asked that he be stripped of his offices and removed from the Governor's counsel. Little was charged generally with inefficiency and dishonesty in office and with improper and highhanded interference in all departments of government. The two specific charges, which were to have serious consequences, were that Little had used his office to extort exorbitant fees and that he had held from the Governor two bills which had "regularly pass'd Both Houses."[29] To the consternation of the Council, Reynolds put into the minutes, along with the remonstrance, Little's reply, which was in part a clever but unconvincing defense and in part a biting counterattack on the individual coun-

25. Minutes of Gov. and Council, Sept. 12, 1755, *Col. Records*, VII, 260.
26. *Ibid.*, 254.   27. *Ibid.*, 261.
28. *Ibid.*, 251-54.   29. *Ibid.*, 254.

cilors, including an uncomplimentary reference to the colonial secretary's spelling.[30] It was only after long delay and at the insistence of the indignant Council, which declared its readiness to prove its charges "in the most Formal Manner,"[31] that Governor Reynolds in the fall created a special court with himself both judge and jury and allowed the councilors to spell out their accusations against Little.[32] Reynolds' verdict, though "clearly of opinion to acquit Mr. Little of every charge," was to remove Little from two of his seven offices for bribetaking, "in order to satisfy his Accusers & the whole Country" of the Governor's "impartiality."[33] After smoldering all summer, the feud between the Council on the one hand and Governor Reynolds and his secretary on the other now burst into open flame. Never again did either make any pretense to confidence in the other. Even the official exchanges between Governor and Council, conventionally couched in terms of extravagant politeness, became almost curt.

Late in November 1755 Reynolds went up to Augusta to meet with the chiefs of the neighboring Creeks. The Governor, acting as the first personal representative of the English King in Georgia, was to bestow a large store of presents from His Majesty on the leading Indians and renew pledges of mutual friendship. Reynolds, who invited two of the less hostile councilors and the colonial secretary, James Habersham, to accompany him and took along William Little in his capacity as commissioner of Indian affairs, departed in a huff when after ten days the chiefs still had not assembled. He left Little behind to speak for him and to distribute the presents, thereby turning over to his private secretary perhaps the single most important task of his administration—that of securing the friendship of the Indian tribes in the vicinity, which, in the absence of military force, could only be won by diplomacy and

30. *Ibid.*, 255-61.
31. Minutes of Gov. and Council, Sept. 30, 1755, *ibid.*, 263.
32. Kellett's Memorial, unpub. Col. Records, XXVII, 273-79.
33. Reynolds' Answer, *ibid.*, XXVIII, Part 1, 187-213.

by the judicious distribution of the presents supplied by the home government.[34]

Little's conference was not an unqualified success. Some of the Indians were unhappy that they were not received by the emissary of the King himself. Many of the old colonists were far from impressed with the naval surgeon's qualifications for treating with the Indians and were not reassured by his failure to consult the superior experience of the councilors who were with him at Augusta. The Board of Trade, displeased that no minutes of the conference were kept, considered Little's 6 per cent commission rather unreasonable.[35]

Preferring to await Little's return from Augusta before calling the General Assembly into session, Reynolds deferred the planned January meeting until February 2, 1756. At that time, he opened the session with an address full of praise for the vigilance of the House on behalf of the government a year before.[36] The House, which had not been in session during the Council's disputes with Reynolds, had no wish to become embroiled in the quarrel. When a message was brought down from the Council on February 3 asking for information concerning the two bills the Council had accused Little of holding up, the House—certainly fully aware of what lay behind the request—took no action on that day and on the next voted down a motion that they answer the Council's message.[37]

Events were moving fast, however, to draw the House into the center of the controversy between Governor and Council. For various reasons only fourteen of the nineteen seats in the Assembly had been filled by February 4 when Charles Watson and Edward Barnard, two of Gray's supporters expelled in the preceding session, were reported elected on writs which Reyn-

34. *Ibid.;* Reynolds to Board of Trade, Jan. 5, 1756, *ibid.,* XXVII, 237-43; Minutes of Gov. and Council, Nov. 7, 1755, *Col. Records,* VII, 294.

35. Minutes of Gov. and Council, Oct. 25, 1757, *Col. Records,* VII, 643-44; Kellett's Memorial, unpub. Col. Records, XXVII, 273-79; Representations of Board of Trade, July 29, 1756, *ibid.,* XXXIV, 171-95.

36. Journal of Upper House, Feb. 2, 1756, *Col. Records,* XVI, 70.

37. Journal of Assembly, Feb. 3-4, 1756, *ibid.,* XIII, 83-89.

olds had issued to fill vacancies occurring during adjournment. Following normal procedure, the speaker turned the warrants of election over to the committee of privileges and elections, which met that afternoon and again the next morning. The point in question was whether the Governor had acted properly in issuing the writs without the request of the House. Before the committee could make its report, a messenger arrived with another note from the Council curtly informing the House that the Council would undertake no further business until it got a reply to its earlier message inquiring about the lost bills. When the House set three o'clock that afternoon as the time for consideration of the Council's request, Reynolds immediately adjourned the legislature until February 12, without explanation.[38]

Upon their return on the twelfth, the assemblymen were met by a tirade from Governor Reynolds in which he berated them for their refusal to admit duly elected members. Declaring that he had adjourned the House for this reason and this reason only, he told them he would consider no action of the House legal as long as Watson and Barnard were denied their seats. The next day, Little as clerk refused to enter anything into the journal until the two new members were admitted. In a defiant mood the House instructed the deputy clerk to keep the journal. At eleven o'clock a message from Reynolds again adjourning the House was snatched from the hand of the speaker who was then forced to remain in his chair until four o'clock while the House completed its answer to the Governor's speech, defending its delay in confirming the election of Barnard and Watson. As soon as the House had assembled for the third time, on February 19, Governor Reynolds called it to the council chamber. After castigating the assemblymen for their refusal to admit Watson and Barnard and for ignoring his message of adjournment, he dissolved the General Assembly.[39]

38. *Ibid.*, 87-91; Journal of Upper House, Feb. 3, 1756, *ibid.*, XVI, 74.
39. Journal of Assembly, *ibid.*, XIII, 91-101.

Exactly what led Reynolds to break with the House, which was filled with men who had proved their influence in the community and their loyalty to him as governor during the Gray affair, was hotly disputed at the time and after. Reynolds steadfastly maintained, even after his return to England, that the refusal of the House to admit duly elected members was the sole reason for the successive adjournments and the final dissolution. The colonial legislators were equally insistent that Reynolds' motive was to prevent any investigation into the conduct of his secretary, William Little. In its report on the Reynolds administration, the Board of Trade in London considered it unlikely that Reynolds would have gone to such extremes to seat two members even before the House had actually disqualified them, especially since their right to the seats was doubtful in the first place. The Board also found it hard to believe that it was only coincidence that the first adjournment came in the nick of time to forestall an investigation into the whereabouts of the "lost bills," which would have led the House straight to Little's doorsteps.[40] Another possible explanation, not canvassed at the time but suggested by future developments, is that Reynolds' political manager, William Little, had already taken over the leadership of the Gray faction to which Barnard and Watson belonged and that one reason for the Governor's insistence upon the House seating the two men was that they had become followers of Mr. Little.

Be that as it may, Governor Reynolds found himself in a most embarrassing predicament in the spring of 1756. The treasury was empty. The tax receipts of the preceding year had fallen far short of expectations and no provision for taxes had been made in the confused session just ended. Reynolds confessed his doubt that he could get an Assembly which would "raise any money for the support of the Government, or even

40. Reynolds to Board of Trade, Mar. 29, 1756, unpub. Col. Records, XXVII, 259-63; Reynolds' Answer, *ibid.*, XXVIII, Part 1, 187-213; Ellis to Board of Trade, Mar. 20, 1757, *ibid.*, 16-17; Kellett's Memorial, *ibid.*, XXVII, 273-79; Representations of Board of Trade, *ibid.*, XXXIV, 171-95.

for holding the Courts of Oyer & Terminer."[41] Nor, of course, could he expect any support from the Council. On the contrary, the recent fiasco in the lower house had encouraged the councilors to make a determined effort to secure his recall. In April, Jonathan Bryan, a councilor and probably the largest landholder in the colony, wrote to Lord Halifax of the "Declining State" of the colony and recommended to him Alexander Kellett for particulars.[42] Kellett, provost marshal and councilor, left for England in the spring of 1756; in July, at the request of "most of the Councillors, Representatives, *Public Officers*, & Planters of Substance & Character" in the colony, he presented to the Commissioners of Trade and Plantations a memorial containing an extremely critical, detailed account of the activities of Reynolds and Little in Georgia.[43] On July 29, 1756, the Board recommended that Reynolds be called back to England to testify and a lieutenant governor be sent out.[44] But it was a long time before word of this got to Georgia,[45] and not until February of the next year did the lieutenant governor, Henry Ellis, arrive to relieve Governor Reynolds.

If up until the summer of 1756 Reynolds deserves a measure of sympathy for the unhappy position into which his political ineptitude and his indiscriminate support of his secretary had led him, from that time to the arrival of Lieutenant Governor Ellis he deserves something very like contempt. No sooner had Kellett left the province than Reynolds suspended him and made his personal steward provost marshal in his stead. After failing to get the senior justice of the general court, Noble Jones, to bar the attorney general from the courtroom, he clashed with Jones until finally, in December 1756, he removed him from both the Council and the court. Another suspension and a resignation cleared the bench; the new general

41. Reynolds to Board of Trade, Mar. 29, 1756, *ibid.*, XXVII, 259-63.
42. Reynolds to Board of Trade, Apr. 6, 1756, *ibid.*, 265.
43. Reynolds to Board of Trade, July 7, 1756, *ibid.*, 273-79.
44. *Ibid.*, XXXIV, 171-95.
45. *S. C. Gaz.*, Oct. 28, 1756.

court of January 1757 was composed of William Little and two of his supporters.[46]

Governor Reynolds showed up in an even worse light at the convening of the new House of Assembly, November 1, 1756. His speech opening the session was a blatant bid for popular support and an obvious move to embarrass the now expected new administration. For nearly two years hardly any money had been coming into the public treasury. In the best of times it got precious little. Yet, with good reason to fear a French-led attack at this time and with no defenses at his command, Reynolds asked only for the re-enactment of the old inadequate tax, with the soothing words that it was "so Easy that Scarce an Individual felt the Weight of it."[47] This was only the first move in Reynolds' ardent courtship of the new House of Assembly and in his campaign to hamstring his replacement. This abrupt change in his dealings with the Assembly from "remarkable haughtiness" to "a conduct quite the reverse" is easily explained:[48] William Little had proved himself a complete success as a campaign manager. Not only had he won an Assembly seat for himself but he had also brought in his chosen followers, including such erstwhile Gray men as Watson, Barnard, Francis, and Marcer. Only four of the old House that had broken with Reynolds were back. The new House promptly made Little its speaker.

With his favorite in firm control of the House of Assembly, Governor Reynolds was content to act as the executive officer of the lower house during his last months in Georgia. In a radical abdication of power he let Little and the House take over the

46. Kellett's Memorial, unpub. Col. Records, XXVII, 273-79; Ellis to Board of Trade, Mar. 11, 1757, *ibid.*, XXVIII, Part 1, 4-15; Minutes of Gov. and Council, Dec. 15-16, 1756, Jan. 14, 17, 1757, *Col. Records*, VII, 450-51, 459-60.

47. Minutes of Gov. and Council, Nov. 1, 1756, *Col. Records*, VII, 413; Journal of Assembly, Jan. 28, 1757, *ibid.*, XIII, 139-41; Journal of Upper House, Nov. 22, 1756, *ibid.*, XVI, 105-6; Reynolds to Board of Trade, May 31, Sept. 22, 1755, Jan. 5, 1756, unpub. Col. Records, XXVII, 151-52, 179-80, 237-43; Ellis to Board of Trade, July 8, Aug. 1, 1757, *ibid.*, XXVIII, Part 1, 42-45, 50-55.

48. Ellis to Board of Trade, Mar. 11, 1757, unpub. Col. Records, XXVIII, Part 1, 4-15.

auditing of public accounts and disbursing of public funds, a function which the governor's commission placed in the hands of the governor in Council. Speaker Little made good use of his supervision of public funds to tighten his control over the Assembly.[49] He also acquiesced in (or perhaps inspired) a resolution of the House which completely exonerated the Gray faction of any wrongdoing at the first sitting of the royal legislature and bluntly accused Reynolds' early advisers of "Bad and Sinister design" in persuading the Governor to oppose Gray.[50]

Before the Christmas recess in 1756, Little appointed a committee to report on the "State of the Province." This report, to serve as a defense of the administration and as an attack on its detractors, was to be adopted by the House and forwarded to the Board of Trade. Its preparation and adoption were the main concerns of the House until Lieutenant Governor Ellis's arrival in February. In preparing its report, the committee met with opposition from the Council (which was unhappy with the turn of things) and particularly from James Habersham, who despite orders from the Governor and various resolutions of the House steadfastly refused to surrender certain official correspondence in his custody. The House finally had to be satisfied with giving him a reprimand, which probably bothered him not at all.[51]

The resolutions adopted by the House on report of its committee laid the blame for the wretched condition of Georgia on the policies pursued by the president and assistants before Reynolds' arrival and on their continued evil influence in colonial affairs as members of the Council. Signed by the representatives of the people and stamped with the seal of the colony, this document Reynolds and Little hoped would carry great weight in their defense. Three weeks before Reynolds gave up the government, someone in the House had the happy

49. Ellis to Board of Trade, May 5, 1757, *ibid.*, 18-31.
50. Journal of Assembly, Jan. 14, 1757, *Col. Records*, XIII, 111.
51. Journal of Assembly, Jan. 18-22, *ibid.*, 114-26.

thought that the speaker, Mr. Little, would soon be going to England. The House decided that nothing could be more appropriate than for him to convey its address to the Lords of Trade and Plantations and "answer all such Questions as they may ask relative thereto."[52] Governor Reynolds, being decidedly of like mind, ordered Little to undertake this chore.

For some time after Ellis had taken over the direction of government, Little and Reynolds remained in Georgia preparing for their day in court. En route home Reynolds was captured by the French and did not reach London until 1757.[53] Then he made his defense and made it as best he could. He was able to point to the "most perfect harmony" existing between himself and the people's representatives for the three months before his leaving Georgia as evidenced by their address brought home by Mr. Little.[54] Nevertheless, the Board thought it desirable for the Governor to return to his ships.

The fact is, Captain Reynolds, who admittedly kept one eye on the promotion board of the Admiralty during his stay in Georgia, never came down from the quarter-deck.[55] Much of his energy was spent on extraordinarily clumsy attempts to make the Council and the House of Assembly a docile crew in his ship of state. Obedience was demanded not for support of some great policy but simply as due the dignity of his office. Occupied with the task of enforcing unquestioning obedience, Reynolds made little headway against the real problems of the colony. He forgot that the office and its powers were his only so long as he used them for the mutual benefit of colony and

52. Journal of Assembly, Feb. 2, 1757, *ibid.*, 152.
53. William Little remained in Georgia until the last of May, 1757 (unpub. Col. Records, XXVIII, Part 1, 46-48). It is uncertain how long Governor Reynolds stayed, but on Mar. 20, 1757, Ellis sent information to the Board of Trade to "account for Mr. Reynolds staying here so long after my arrival" (*ibid.*, 16-17). The *South-Carolina Gazette*, in an item dated Feb. 17, 1757, stated that Reynolds had taken passage on a ship then loading in Midway River. Reynolds seems to have arrived in London on July 7, 1757 (unpub. Col. Records, XXVIII, Part 1, 188); but he did not announce his arrival until Oct. 14, 1757 (*ibid.*, 95), and his defense was not received by the Board until Mar. 6, 1758.
54. Reynolds' Answer, unpub. Col. Records, XXVIII, Part 1, 187-213.
55. Minutes of Gov. and Council, Sept. 12, 1755, *Col. Records*, VII, 253.

king. When it became apparent to both that such was not the case, he was removed.

John Reynolds' failure to win the support of the colonists had other and less happy consequences than returning to His Majesty's Navy its own. The House of Assembly, the Council, the Board of Trade, and Governor Reynolds himself were in agreement that all was not well with the colony of Georgia. It was, they concurred, in a "declining State": no people of substance had lately come into it, many had left it and were leaving it daily, and little or no trade was being carried on. Where they failed to agree was upon the causes of the trouble. Aside from the unconvincing argument that it was due to malicious advice from councilors set on bringing Governor Reynolds to ruin at any cost, the main contention of Reynolds and his friends was that the war and the consequent unwillingness of settlers to come to an unprotected frontier were the root of the difficulty. Reynolds' opponents, whom the Board of Trade supported, agreed in part but maintained that, just as important, settlement in Georgia was made unattractive for men of property by the Governor's mistreatment and neglect of the leading men of the colony.

What both overlooked and what becomes immediately evident in the light of Ellis's subsequent success was that Governor Reynolds' unfortunate political activities had prevented his taking the lead in measures to nourish and strengthen the colony. The factional fights and animosities of these two and one-half years made impossible the constructive political action which alone could, and in time did, save it from the dangers of disintegration or destruction. Here is the true measure of Reynolds' failure as a colonial administrator. As the great war which had complicated Reynolds' entire administration developed and spread, Governor Reynolds had repeated warnings from Lord Loudoun and from the Governor of South Carolina of impending attacks from the Indians and even of invasion by the French from the West Indies. At such times, more was needed than laments over the poverty and weakness of the colony followed by humble requests for aid. But instead of drawing closer to South Carolina in his peril, Reynolds had irritated the Governor of that colony by fretting over such trifles as the delivery of his mail. Instead of moving heaven and earth to keep the friendship of the Indians, he had wrapped the dignity of his office about him and stalked out of his one important meeting with them. Instead of seeking to unite the weak and exposed colony under his leadership, he had reduced it to a mess of squabbling factions. When the war broke out Reynolds had not one adequate fort at his disposal, but he made no move to erect fortifications or to effect repairs. He did raise a troop of forty Rangers shortly before his departure, but only at the Council's insistence and without providing for its support. And he did on occasion support the colonists in their attempts to relieve the crippling shortage of currency and he helped them get a more workable land policy, both of which were important.

But plainly Reynolds never had any broad plan for attacking the problems of the colony, and just as plainly he lacked the political sense and the character to carry through any such plan had it existed. In the main he allowed the colony to drift, and it drifted to the rim of disaster. Yet, from the failure of the Reynolds administration the leading men of the colony learned of the need for cooperation between governor and colonist if the colony were to prosper; from their success in routing Reynolds and Little, they learned something about their ability to oppose a governor and policies they disliked. Both lessons they were to put to good use.

CHAPTER III

Governor Henry Ellis,
1757-1760

HENRY ELLIS, an odd and rather wonderful Englishman, arrived in Georgia in 1757 to replace John Reynolds. For three years he governed the colony, leaving in 1760. His three years as governor were but an interlude, and a short one, in an extraordinarily varied and colorful career. Yet Ellis's stay in Georgia is what makes him something more than simply an eighteenth-century English gentleman of rare charm and intelligence. For one time in a long life this gifted dilettante was faced with a situation which demanded the full play of his powers. As a result, a really first-rate talent for politics and diplomacy bloomed briefly in Georgia. It was Ellis's skill as a politician and diplomat, and little else, that protected a part of the remote southern flank of Britain's American empire at a critical juncture in the last and the greatest of the French and Indian wars.

The spectacle of Henry Ellis, the Royal Governor of the province, walking at midday along the sandy streets of Savannah during the unusually hot summer of 1758 with a thermometer dangling by a thread from his umbrella to "the height of his nostrils," must have lingered long in the memories of the Savannah townspeople.[1] Their perspiring Governor was in fact only displaying for all to see certain facets of his personality—his avid curiosity, his lively and lifelong interest

1. Henry Ellis, "An Account of the Heat of the Weather in Georgia . . . ," *London Mag.* (1759), 371-72.

in all natural phenomena, his passion for exact scientific data, and, incidentally, his "rational, benevolent, and pleasant" "singularities in character."[2] In this particular instance, Ellis, an old tropical hand and veteran of the Guinea trade, was astounded to discover from his thermometer that it was "highly possible" that the inhabitants of Savannah breathed "a hotter air than any other people on the face of the earth."[3]

Governor Ellis had been indulging this penchant for observing the oddities of nature in foreign places for many years before coming to Georgia. Born in 1721, he had run away in his early youth and gone to sea. For a number of years he led the life of a sailor. His whereabouts were unknown to his family during this time, but eventually a reconciliation between father and son took place. The elder Ellis thereafter actively promoted the career of his son and at his death left him an estate which made Henry Ellis a wealthy man.[4]

Before he was thirty-five years old Ellis had seen much of the world. Although most of his voyages were to the tropics— three to equatorial Africa and three to the West Indies—his most famous was to the polar regions. In 1746, as a young man of twenty-five and evidently by now once again enjoying the patronage of his father, he returned to England from Italy just in time to learn that an expedition was on the point of sailing for Hudson Bay in search of a northwest passage to Asia. Hearing of his interest in the project, the magnates who were financing the voyage sent for Ellis and offered him command of one of the ships, even though a captain had already been chosen. Ellis refused the appointment because of his insufficient experience with "Northern Seas and Northern Climates" and, instead, became himself a patron of the expedition and a passenger on one of the ships. The explorers failed to discover

2. Lord Gardenstone, *Travelling Anecdotes*, quoted in John Nichols, *Literary Anecdotes of the Eighteenth Century* (London, 1812-15), IX, 533.

3. Ellis, "An Account . . . ," *London Mag.* (1759), 371-72.

4. John Nichols, *Illustrations of the Literary History of the Eighteenth Century* (London, 1817-58), I, 477.

the Northwest Passage, but the expedition provided Ellis with the opportunity for writing a book, on the strength of which he was made a fellow of the Royal Society. In his book Ellis takes note of everything in the heavens above and the earth beneath. And he speculates about everything that he observes, particularly the temperature. His deductions and conclusions are always logical, plausible, stimulating, and delivered with clarity and pungency. Unfortunately they are nearly always mistaken.[5]

A decade later, in Georgia, Ellis applied these same powers of observation to the political scene. Happily, in this instance the conclusions that he drew with his usual logic and imagination were nearly always correct. He was a better politician than scientist, although to both pursuits he brought pace and style. Henry Ellis landed in Charleston on the twenty-seventh day of January 1757, his commission as lieutenant governor of Georgia in hand. He had decided to stop there instead of going directly to Savannah because he was anxious to get "advice and information" from Mr. Lyttelton, the Governor of South Carolina, before plunging into the bitter political controversy which he knew awaited him in Georgia. Always alert to exploit every possibility in a situation, he took this opportunity to conciliate the South Carolina Governor and to arrange for a regular correspondence, which continued uninterrupted until both men departed America in 1760. The two hit it off well from the beginning. In his letters Ellis always took pains to defer to Lyttelton as Governor of the important province upon which the welfare of Georgia in so many ways depended, although he sometimes chafed under the necessity of following in Lyttelton's wake; and he did not hesitate to press the claims of Georgia with his colleague when he felt it proper for him to do so. Ellis's crackling performance as Governor of Georgia on occasion evoked from Lyttelton a testy letter

5. Henry Ellis, *A Voyage to Hudson's-Bay, by the Dobbs Galley and California, in the Years 1746 and 1747, for Discovering a North West Passage* . . . (Dublin, 1749), 48-50.

betraying displeasure at his lack of respect for the senior
partner; but Ellis's main aim was accomplished.[6]

The weather in Charleston being bad, Ellis dallied until
the eleventh of February before leaving for Beaufort, where he
embarked in one of the South Carolina scout boats on the
fifteenth. Arriving at Savannah on the next day, he was met
on the bluff by "loud Huzza's" from the inhabitants.[7] The
"tumultuous demonstrations of joy" that followed filled the
detached and observant young Englishman with wry amuse-
ment,[8] and he was not unduly impressed when the citizenry
that night placed upon an enormous bonfire an effigy of "a
certain Tyrant in himself, a Promoter of it in his Master, and
his greatest Enemy"—Mr. William Little, Reynolds' crony.[9]
Ellis took his oath of office, ordered all officials to carry on as
usual, and, "finding a recess would be agreeable at this Season
of the Year," "thought it prudent" to adjourn the legislature
immediately. After he had removed two of Reynolds' most
recent nominees to the Council with "such apparent justice &
impartiality that no umbrage was taken even by these Gentlemen,"[10] Ellis played a waiting game while the storm raged
about him. The men who had lost out under Reynolds, hungry
for revenge and for office, set up a clamor for the new Governor
to turn the old lot out. Ellis listened; he sympathized and
soothed. He took the measure of his would-be friends and of
his political opponents. From what he read and heard, he
learned and began to understand. But he did nothing; he
promised nothing.

Sensible of my own inexperience & of the violence of such
Councils fearful of being misled & aiming rather at healing

6. Ellis to Board of Trade, Mar. 11, 1757, unpub. Col. Records, XXVIII,
Part 1, 4-15; Lyttelton Papers, Clements Lib.
7. *S. C. Gaz.*, Apr. 28, 1757, and Jan. 6, 27, Mar. 17, 1757.
8. Ellis to Lyttelton, Feb. 18, 1757, Lyttelton Papers, Clements Lib.
9. *S. C. Gaz.*, Apr. 28, 1757, and Jan. 6, 27, Mar. 17, 1757.
10. Ellis to Board of Trade, Mar. 11, 1757, unpub. Col. Records, XXVIII,
Part 1, 4-15; Minutes of Gov. and Council, Feb. 16-17, 1757, *Col. Records*,
VII, 485-91.

the wounds and extinguishing the flame of Party than stirring it anew, I forebore making any material alteration until I should be qualified to Act from observation & experience in order that the Changes I shall then make may rather be attributed to my own judgment than to the advice of designing and interested people.—This suspense will give time for mens passions to subside & for truth to appear through the cloud of party prejudice that at present obscures it.[11]

While friend and foe alike were waiting for the new Governor to show his hand, Ellis was taking a hard look at Georgia and analyzing what he saw. Immediately he perceived that it was essential to devise ways and means for bolstering the defenses of the colony. Despite distractions of every sort, Ellis never once forgot that every consideration, no matter how attractive or desirable, had always to give way before the great need for building up the defensive strength of the province.[12]

But there was one problem even more immediate. First of all, the political tangle left by Reynolds had to be unraveled. Ellis was fully aware that he must gain the support of all the inhabitants before he could do much toward reviving the colony —even the most strenuous efforts of all the settlers would hardly suffice to make Georgia strong, the colony being as small and poor as it was. Ellis wisely let time work for him in erasing the passions and bitter feelings which Reynolds had left behind, but soon he began unobtrusively and quietly a campaign to reconcile the differences which split the colony into rival factions and to bring the supporters of Reynolds and Little into his camp. Using restraint, treating all fairly and without prejudice, advocating nothing but what was obviously for the general good, he rallied the colony to his support with a deft and sure political touch. Before summer was far gone, harmony reigned.

Ellis quickly grasped the elemental political fact, which had

11. Ellis to Board of Trade, Mar. 11, 1757, unpub. Col. Records, XXVIII, Part 1, 4-15.
12. Ellis to Lyttelton, Apr. 1757, Lyttelton Papers, Clements Lib.

eluded Reynolds, that the Council was the governor's natural ally in colonial politics. Made up of the most substantial men in the colony and appointed on the recommendation of the governor, the Council offered a substantial foundation on which the governor could build. The elected House of Assembly could be courted and bent to the governor's will, but because it had another master, could never be completely depended upon.

From the first Ellis treated the members of his Council with great deference and respect. He was meticulous in consulting them on all matters of public interest, not only to win their support but because he recognized their superior experience in colonial affairs and valued their advice. During the spring of 1757, by keeping the Council busy with affairs of state he filled its members with a gratifying sense of their own importance.[13] If this unwonted attention were not enough to win over the wariest councilor, Ellis's approach to the Indian problem secured the enthusiastic approval of these old frontiersmen and made of them his warmest supporters.

While wooing the Council, Governor Ellis was also patching up the weaknesses in the position left him, intentionally or otherwise, by his predecessor. He set out to regain the powers and prerogatives of the governor which Reynolds had allowed to slip away in his open bid for popular favor during the last days of his administration. Ellis was least willing to countenance the legislature's assumption of the right to audit and pay the public accounts.[14] Not one to make a frontal assault when indirection would serve, Ellis, calling the Council together while the legislature was still recessed, told them that Speaker Little's policy of playing favorites in paying accounts had so damaged public credit that it had to be remedied at once and suggested that they advertise for all holders of public accounts to present them for payment. With this one stroke he repaired

13. Minutes of Gov. and Council, *Col. Records*, VII, 498-501, 539, 543-45, 610.

14. Ellis to Board of Trade, Jan. 1, 1758, May 5, 1757, unpub. Col. Records, XXVIII, Part 1, 144-47, 18-31.

the colony's credit, pleased its creditors, and restored the disbursement of public funds to the governor and Council—and all without any overt challenge to the House.[15]   Ellis was also displeased to learn that Reynolds had gone so far as to request the House of Assembly to nominate the new justices of the peace.   Consequently, in March, he issued a new commission of the peace, adding new names but carefully including most of the old ones.   By this move Ellis pleased some while offending few, if any, and effectively reasserted the governor's right to commission justices without consulting the Assembly.[16]

Ellis complained bitterly that Reynolds before his departure had seen to it that "every publick Office that either existed or were likely to be established, were filled with his Creatures," even to the staffing of two troops of Rangers which existed only on paper.   On May 5 Ellis tells how he got around this in the case of the militia officers:

I have just been Regimenting the Militia. . .—This step afforded me an opportunity of gratifying some worthy men, who are vain of Military Titles, of putting the Militia in a condition of being useful & I may add of establishing a right that Mr. Reynolds intended giving up to the Assembly that of appointing the Officers.[17]

And incidentally the officers were indebted for their commissions to Governor Ellis, not to Reynolds.   William Little's impending departure did leave vacant a place on the general court, and, although Ellis distrusted the two remaining justices and suspected that they, with Little, were in collusion with the notorious Bosomworths who were seeking judicial validation of their claim to three of the islands off the Georgia coast, he chose not to disturb them.   Instead, in view of the "Business of great

15. Minutes of Gov. and Council, Apr. 4, 20, 1757, *Col. Records*, VII, 507, 545; Ellis to Board of Trade, Aug. 1, 1757, unpub. Col. Records, XXVIII, Part 1, 50-55.

16. Ellis to Board of Trade, Mar. 11, 1757, unpub. Col. Records, XXVIII, Part 1, 4-15; Journal of Assembly, Feb. 1, 1757, *Col. Records*, XIII, 145-46; Minutes of Gov. and Council, Mar. 29, 1757, *ibid.*, VII, 504-5.

17. Ellis to Board of Trade, May 5, Mar. 11, 1757, unpub. Col. Records, XXVIII, Part 1, 18-31, 4-15.

Importance to come before the ensuing Court," Ellis persuaded the Council that not one but three new justices should be appointed, thereby giving his appointees a majority on the bench.[18]

By far the knottiest problem left Ellis by Reynolds and Little was the hostility of their hand-picked House of Assembly. Ellis became acutely aware on the very day of his arrival at Savannah that he would have to be "very circumspect" in dealing with the lower house of the legislature.[19] A "private Society" greeted him on the bluff with a paper asking him to dissolve the Assembly,[20] and he soon learned that plans were afoot in every district of the colony to forward similar addresses to the Governor. Simultaneously he found out that the Assembly "at the instance of Mr Little their Speaker" intended to address him in such a manner as would put him in a false position should he choose to call for new elections. It was at this point that Ellis decided that it would be "prudent" to adjourn the Assembly for a month, and he found it "expedient" to extend the prorogations through the spring.[21]

Early in March, while Ellis was busy writing a long letter to England giving his first impressions of Georgia, William Little, the former speaker, called on the new Governor and "among other things" dared Ellis to dissolve the Assembly, declaring it would be futile "as he had taken measures to have the same men rechosen." Ellis refused to be smoked out by these taunts but continued to gather together the strings of his power against the day when he would have to have a showdown with Mr. Little's Assembly.[22]

Ellis pondered whether to form a new legislature, which certainly would be easier to handle, or to stick with the old and

18. Minutes of Gov. and Council, Mar. 29, 1757, *Col. Records*, VII, 504; Ellis to Board of Trade, Mar. 11, 1757, unpub. Col. Records, XXVIII, Part 1, 4-15; Ellis to Lyttelton, Apr. 1757, Lyttelton Papers, Clements Lib.
19. Ellis to Board of Trade, Mar. 11, 1757, unpub. Col. Records, XXVIII, Part 1, 4-15.
20. Ellis's notation on William Little to House of Assembly, May 25, 1757, *ibid.*, 46-48.
21. Ellis to Board of Trade, Mar. 11, 1757, *ibid.*, 4-15.
22. *Ibid.*

try to win it to his side. Ellis's policy during these crucial first three or four months was clearly designed not to build up a following which could overpower the Reynolds faction but rather to conciliate the men indebted to Reynolds so that the whole colony would join with him in working out its problems. He looked on Little's friends in the Assembly as ordinary men, "flexible weak & ignorant," "not dishonest in their private characters but easy credulous & equally disposed to good or evil." The only real fault he could find in them was that they were inclined to oppose him in order to justify "their friends lately in power," which Ellis considered reasonable enough under the circumstances. He remained steadfast in his opinion that if he offered only what was "most apparently for their own good," they would prove "more tractable" than was generally imagined. "But if they should be obstinate or fractiously inclined," he wrote, "I think a way is to be found of getting rid of them without appearing to act from resentments": he would make the formation of a new legislature mandatory simply by ordering the wished-for division of the colony into parishes.[23]

All during the spring of 1757 Ellis was taking great pains to get acquainted with the people of the colony and mapping out his plan of action to suit it to their "disposition."[24] By the first of May he had decided to call the old legislature back into session on June 16. Then it was that the details of Mr. Little's plot came out into the open. When he departed for London late in May, Little left with a local planter, Mr. Patrick Mackay, a letter for the members of the Assembly giving them thinly disguised instructions to maintain their opposition to the Council and new Governor at all costs.[25] The plan was for Mackay to get Little's seat in the House where he would be elected speaker, and then head a junto to be formed for the sole

23. *Ibid.;* Ellis to Lyttelton, June 22, 1757, Lyttelton Papers, Clements Lib.
24. Ellis to Board of Trade, May 5, 1757, unpub. Col. Records, XXVIII, Part 1, 18-31.
25. William Little to House of Assembly, May 25, 1757, *ibid.,* 46-48; Ellis to Lyttelton, May 1, June 22, 1757, Lyttelton Papers, Clements Lib.

purpose of blocking anything that Ellis should advocate. It was expected that the disorders arising from the ensuing stalemate would afford the legislature the occasion for petitioning the King to retain Mr. Reynolds in office. When Ellis got word of what was intended, he acted swiftly and effectively. Because of the Governor's determination "to discountenance his being elected," Mackay, Ellis reported, "lost the election," and "is retired with disgust and disappointment to his plantation."[26] With justified satisfaction and a touch of arrogance Ellis tells how he put a stop to this affair before it was well started:

I have totally frustrated, and disconcerted a conspiracy that was formed under the late Administration, to disturb mine, by obstructing all my measures.—Some I have conquered by address, and others by a seasonable, and spirited opposition, and resentment.[27]

With the defeat of Mackay all organized opposition to Ellis disappeared, never again to plague him as long as he stayed in Georgia. Hereafter the colonists, almost to a man, were Ellis men. Even the House of Assembly fell into line so completely that during its first session the House often seemed to be vying with the Council in its efforts to please the Governor. Nothing "that I proposed to them," Ellis later declared of the first session, "that was not done, and in the very way I would have it. . . ."[28]

It is difficult to see how Ellis could have done better during his first few months in Georgia. His political technique seems faultless. A keen sense of timing allowed him to act with an economy of motion that made every move count for much; an almost impersonal detachment enabled him to disarm his enemies without giving offense and to bare his fist only when policy, not pique, dictated. The smallness of the constituency

26. Ellis to Board of Trade, July 8, 1757, Feb. 10, 1759, unpub. Col. Records, XXVIII, Part 1, 42-45, 260-64.
27. Ellis to Lyttelton, July 8, 1757, Lyttelton Papers, Clements Lib.
28. Ellis to Lyttelton, July 20, 1757, Jan. 21, 1758, *ibid.*

does not alter the fact that a difficult and delicate situation had been handled with political artistry. Ellis without modesty but with truth summed up his accomplishments of the spring of 1757: ". . . By address, by bold, but honest arts, & by doing my duty in a way unusual here, I have at length been able to change the temper of my opponents to my wishes."[29]

This virtuoso performance gains meaning from the fact that behind the political maneuvers lay a purpose. All during this first spring Governor Ellis's mind was continually ranging over the possibilities open to him for giving new life and strength to this colony which had gained precious little of either in the past twenty-five years. Here too he moved slowly at the outset.

I have a variety of designs in my own mind which have for their object the utility and happiness of this Colony.—But perhaps it would be premature to enter upon them before I am qualified to judge of their practicability & whether they are well or ill adapted to our Circumstances.—This knowledge can only be derived from experience & that requires time.[30]

But Ellis was ready with his plan of attack when he called the legislature into session. The bills which he prepared for consideration were designed to blunt the three-pronged predicament which had the colony pinned to the wall. Inadequate defenses, insufficient wealth, and too few settlers were keeping Georgia small, poor, and weak. Since the solution of each waited upon the solution of both the others, Ellis's legislative program[31] was rather like a formula for lifting oneself by one's own bootstraps and was of necessity limited in its aims. For the next three years the Governor, using whatever came to hand, devoted his considerable energy, intelligence, and even a part of his personal fortune, to bringing his colony more men, greater wealth, and a stronger defense.

29. Ellis to Board of Trade, July 8, 1757, unpub. Col. Records, XXVIII, Part 1, 42-45.
30. Ellis to Board of Trade, Mar. 11, 1757, *ibid.*, 4-15.
31. Ellis to Lyttelton, July 8, 1757, Lyttelton Papers, Clements Lib.

Ellis's first concern was to provide the inhabitants with some measure of security from Indian attack.

To this weakness & insecurity may in a great measure be imputed the little progress this Colony has made . . . for in a Country that is exposed to every kind of outrage & injustice within & to every sort of depredation & attack how can we expect that people will trust themselves or their property? incessantly uneasy incessantly in alarm no person that has anything to lose or is exempt from the terrors of a Jail will come among us.[32]

Realizing that no funds could possibly be forthcoming for a military establishment in 1757, Governor Ellis made the ingenious proposal to the legislature that the labor traditionally given by all the inhabitants to road work be diverted to the building of wooden stockades at key spots about the colony.[33] The one fortification standing in Georgia at the time was the old fort at Augusta, which was in a state of such advanced decay that the guns had to be trundled out of the building on the King's birthday lest the firing bring the structure's complete collapse.[34]   In August and September 1757, the men of the colony worked for twelve days putting a palisade around the town of Savannah and building one log fort to the north of Augusta and three south of Savannah.   By the end of September all of the forts were completed or near completion, and Savannah's palisade was manned with old guns dug up out of the sand on the bluff.[35]

Georgia, Ellis knew, could not place its main reliance for protection on the strength of its own arms, but he was unremitting in his labors to make the local defense establishment as

32. Ellis to Board of Trade, Mar. 11, 1757, unpub. Col. Records, XXVIII, Part 1, 4-15; Ellis to Loudoun, Feb. 28, 1757, Amherst Papers, Lib. Cong.

33. Ellis to Board of Trade, May 5, 1757, unpub. Col. Records, XXVIII, Part 1, 18-31; Minutes of Gov. and Council, Mar. 14, 1757, *Col. Records*, VII, 498-99; Journal of Assembly, June 16, 1757, *ibid.*, XIII, 171; Ellis to Lyttelton, Apr. 1757, Lyttelton Papers, Clements Lib.

34. Reynolds to Board of Trade, Jan. 5, 1756, unpub. Col. Records, XXVII, 237-243; Reynolds to Loudoun, July 23, 1756, Amherst Papers, Lib. Cong.

35. Ellis to Board of Trade, Aug. 1, Sept. 20, 1757, unpub. Col. Records, XXVIII, Part 1, 50-55, 92-94.

strong as conditions would permit. Naturally he never ceased to importune British military authorities and the Board of Trade for troops and equipment; but, long before the legislature returned to Savannah, he was also working to enable Georgia to make some show of military power on its own. As a beginning, he already had the troop of forty Rangers which Reynolds had recently raised, but no provision had been made for its support. Since the colony lacked the means to pay for such a force, Ellis had the choice of disbanding the company or of taking upon himself the responsibility for paying the troopers. He chose to keep the Rangers, and by using various stratagems he held the troop together. He also put the remaining able-bodied men into a new militia organization and demanded equipment for them from Britain. When the muskets he had requested arrived, he did not hesitate to issue them to individual militiamen.[36]

Ellis's persistence in demanding that regular British troops be stationed in Georgia soon bore fruit. Ellis announced to the Assembly in July that he had wrung a promise from the commanding officer of the King's forces in South Carolina for "a small Body of Troops" and that one hundred men would be sent if Georgia would agree to pay for their transport and provide weekly rations. Ignoring the Assembly's declaration that it would be utterly impossible for the colony to subsist such a body of men, Ellis gave instructions for the detachment to be sent ahead, which was done.[37]

With the arrival of the Virginia Regiment of Blues, Governor Ellis might well have taken time out for self-congratulation. As a matter of fact, he was discouraged. The defenses of

36. Ellis to Board of Trade, Mar. 11, May 5, 25, 1757, *ibid.*, 4-15, 18-31, 36-39; Ellis to Pitt, Aug. 1, 1757, *ibid.*, 57-60; Minutes of Gov. and Council, Mar. 25, July 4, 1757, Nov. 17, 21, 1758, *Col. Records*, VII, 503, 600, 842, 845-46; Ellis to Lyttelton, Feb. 18, June 23, July 8, 1757, Lyttelton Papers, Clements Lib.; Ellis to Loudoun, Feb. 28, 1757, ff., Amherst Papers, Lib. Cong.

37. Journal of Assembly, July 19, 1757, *Col. Records*, XIII, 220-21; Ellis to Board of Trade, Sept. 20, 1757, unpub. Col. Records, XXVIII, Part 1, 92-94.

the colony were still far from adequate, and he realized that he could proceed no further along these lines, however great the need, until he had induced new settlers to come in. Only an enlarged and productive population could provide the men and funds for further expanding the colonial defense establishment. These considerations made Ellis careful to set against the always urgent need for defense funds the advantages of keeping taxes to a minimum so that the embryo merchant or planter could prosper, pay his creditors in South Carolina, and so increase the productivity and trade of the colony. This in turn would lead other men of means and ability to settle, and in time Georgia would reach the point where it no longer had to cringe before its enemies. Consequently Ellis concluded that the welfare of the colony would best be served in the long run by his putting the prosperity of the inhabitants first, whenever the requirements of defense would possibly permit.[38]

Although determined to keep taxes low, Ellis knew the importance of placing public finance on as sound a footing as possible. The second request that he made of the legislature in the summer of 1757 was for it to provide for bridging the gap between the public debt of £850 and the £260 in ordinary revenue, which Reynolds' "improvident administration" had left him.[39] The Assembly renewed the general tax on land and slaves at double the old rate. Ellis, while admitting that even this would hardly bring in more than £500, defended it as proof that there was "every disposition that could be wished in the people to answer the most sanguine expectations, but they really are incapable of doing more than they have done. . . ."[40] To aid the legislature in making the annual tax levy, Ellis instituted the practice of submitting to the House each year an estimate of expected expenditures. He wisely left it to the

38. Ellis to Board of Trade, Mar. 11, Aug. 1, 1757, Apr. 24, 1759, Aug. 25, 1760, unpub. Col. Records, XXVIII, Part 1, 4-15, 50-55, 291-303, 456-59.
39. Ellis to Board of Trade, July 8, 1757, *ibid.*, 42-45.
40. Ellis to Pitt, Aug. 1, 1757, *ibid.*, 57-60; Ellis to Lyttelton, Apr. 1757, Lyttelton Papers, Clements Lib.

representatives to decide each year how heavy a tax rate the people could bear.

The legislature also passed in the summer of 1757 a bill providing for the printing and emission of £630 in paper currency. This measure was designed to help refund the public debt, to provide credit, and to put into circulation much-needed specie. For years the unfavorable balance of trade against Georgia and the payments made by many of her settlers to creditors in South Carolina had combined to drain off all of the colony's specie. If the Assembly had not taken steps to provide some means of exchange, it would have been almost impossible for the colony to carry on business, public or private. On this both Governor Reynolds and Governor Ellis were agreed. However, the Governor's Instructions specifically forbade him to allow the printing of paper bills without the permission of the Board of Trade, and the Board was not inclined to give its permission. Although a bill passed in 1755 which put £7000 in paper currency into circulation had still not been approved, Ellis rescued this currency from devaluation by accepting it in payment of public fees. And he approved the new money bill.[41] When the Board of Trade reprimanded Ellis for accepting the old bills as legal tender and for permitting a new issue of paper money,[42] he apologized, and then made a cogent argument in favor of paper currency:

As the Money lent to the planters was at a low interest they found their advantage in investing it in Negroes the labour of whom not only served to improve the lands but added also to the export of the province and thereby diminished the Balance of Trade against it. And the Revenue arising from the Interest paid for the use of that money enabled the Government to undertake several important and necessary services without any additional burthen to the people.—A burthen that they would

41. Ellis to Board of Trade, Apr. 24, 1759, unpub. Col. Records, XXVIII, Part 1, 291-303.
42. Board of Trade to Ellis, Apr. 21, 1758, *ibid.*, XXXIV, 220-36.

have been still less able to bear had they been deprived of the profit arising from the money lent them. . . .[43]

The money remained in circulation.

The third bill which Ellis prepared for the Assembly meeting in June and July 1757 was aimed directly at the problem of attracting settlers. It was designed to draw into Georgia some of the less fortunate men living in the colonies to the north or on the islands of the West Indies. In effect, it promised protection for any debtor from his creditor if he could get across the Savannah River without being caught, unless the creditor happened to be a South Carolinian. This was also a move by Ellis in the game between him and his able Spanish adversary at St. Augustine for the allegiance of Edmund Gray and his followers who had settled in the disputed territory lying between the English and Spanish colonies.[44]

Less fanciful were Ellis's efforts to make good land available for newcomers. The securing of land grants was already easy and simple. What Ellis feared was that it was so easy that a small number of men would gradually build up enormous holdings. He argued that the supply of good land was strictly limited by the treaties with the Indians, which confined the colony to the tidelands and the environs of the Savannah River, and that unless some land were reserved for new settlers, Georgia would never have the white men needed for the defense of the frontier.[45] After winning the Board's approval of an act declaring vacant all old grants which had not been taken up,[46] Ellis continued to insist that a limit should be placed on family holdings so that frontier Georgia would become a colony of middle-sized farms with a large white population instead of a colony of large plantations with a large slave popu-

43. Ellis to Board of Trade, Apr. 24, 1759, *ibid.*, XXVIII, Part 1, 291-303.

44. Ellis to Board of Trade, May 5, 1757, *ibid.*, 18-31; Journal of Assembly, *Col. Records*, XIII, 171; Ellis to Lyttelton, May 1, undated [late May?], 1757, Lyttelton Papers, Clements Lib.

45. Ellis to Board of Trade, Mar. 20, May 5, 1757, Apr. 24, 1759, unpub. Col. Records, XXVIII, Part 1, 16-17, 18-31, 291-303.

46. Board of Trade to Ellis, Apr. 21, 1758, *ibid.*, XXXIV, 220-36.

lation. When the Board of Trade informed Ellis that it was not interested in the size of the holdings but rather in their productivity, Ellis's reply attests to his political sophistication and suggests a moral that rulers of an empire might well ponder:

. . . that system of policy which may be proper for the middle provinces upon this Continent is not for those upon the frontier. —The first object with the former is the increase of produce and extension of Commerce.—In the latter it should be security & defence.—The former are secured from danger by their situation[;] the latter exposed to it from the same circumstance[.] the first might have more indulgencies of one kind[;] the last more of another.[47]

Thus it was that Governor Ellis set in motion his colonial policy in 1757. His general approach was marked out in the legislation of that summer. For the next three years he pushed his attack upon Georgia's predicament on all three fronts. But Ellis knew full well he was living in a fool's paradise with his projects and plans so long as the Indians might any fine day descend upon the settlements murdering the unwary and sending the fainthearted flying for South Carolina. Unable to rely on force alone to defend his province, Governor Ellis adopted the wiles of diplomacy to hold back the forces of the natives and to neutralize the influence of the Spanish and French in the area. Relations with the Indians absorbed most of Ellis's attention after 1757, and it was as a diplomat that Ellis made his most valuable contribution to the colony and displayed his greatest talent.

The *sine qua non* of Ellis's diplomacy was the retention of at least the outward forms of friendship between the Creek Indians and the English. By making great display of what little military strength the colony had and by encouraging the impression that the strength of South Carolina and the strength of Georgia were inseparable, he sought to persuade the Creeks

47. Ellis to Board of Trade, Apr. 24, 1759, *ibid.*, XXVIII, Part 1, 291-303.

of the foolhardiness of arousing the ire of the whites in Georgia. The annual allotment of presents for the Indians and the mutually profitable trade between the Creeks and the colonists he held out as the strongest inducements for them to continue on good relations with the English settlers. Realizing that it would be useless or even dangerous to attempt to force the Creeks to break completely with the French, he never missed an opportunity to lessen the French influence in favor of the English, always picturing in the blackest terms French cruelty and French treachery as opposed to the kindness and good faith of the English. As for his dealings with the Spanish—who had never been particularly successful in their relations with the Indians—Governor Ellis did what he could to keep alive the "deep rooted aversion" felt by the Creeks for the men of Spain, all the while keeping up a ceremonious correspondence with the Spanish Governor of Florida and maintaining a "discreet and very delicate conduct, always adapted to the circumstances" of the moment.[48] Any disagreement or misunderstanding arising between the Creeks and the Cherokee he considered a boon, and he assiduously encouraged any quarrels within the tribes. The success of his policy is suggested by the fact that despite times of great tension Georgia was never actually attacked while Ellis was Governor, even when the neighboring South Carolina frontier was laid waste by the Cherokee.[49]

Georgia had had an Indian scare in the early fall of 1756, shortly before Ellis's arrival, when white settlers had murdered two Creeks near Augusta. Everything was beginning to quiet down when Ellis took office; and as soon as the Indians got news that a new governor had come to Savannah they began to drift into town singly and in groups to see Ellis and to hint for

48. Ellis to Board of Trade, Oct. 22, May 5, Nov. 25, 1757, July 26, 1759, *ibid.*, 97-101, 18-31, 114-17, 306-10; Minutes of Gov. and Council, Sept. 13, 1757, *Col. Records*, VII, 626; Ellis to Lyttelton, May 1, Sept. 5, Nov. 11, 1757, Lyttelton Papers, Clements Lib.

49. Ellis to Lyttelton, Sept. 24, 1757, ff., Lyttelton Papers, Clements Lib.; Ellis to Amherst, Oct. 5, 1759, ff., Amherst Papers, Lib. Cong.

presents. Governor Ellis never failed to receive them with ceremony and politeness. In a year's time he entertained nearly thirteen hundred Indians at his home or in his chambers. Though he came to be widely known and greatly admired for his skill and finesse in treating with the Indians, Ellis sometimes found the Indian spokesmen quite as adept as he in the art of blending the honeyed word with the veiled threat.[50]

When the Indian presents were brought up the river to Savannah on May 18, 1757, Governor Ellis wrote to Governor Lyttelton in Charleston, who had never met the Creek chiefs, suggesting that they jointly call a congress of the headmen of the Creeks and distribute the presents.[51] The advantages of identifying Georgia with South Carolina in the minds of the Indians, Ellis felt, far outweighed any loss of personal prestige which might result from his playing second fiddle to the Governor of South Carolina.[52] Governor Lyttelton replied that he had already invited the chiefs to Charleston and suggested the Indians come by Savannah on their return. Ellis readily agreed. On July 20 he got an appropriation of twenty pounds from the Assembly to pay for sending his agent to the Creeks to invite their leaders to a conference in Savannah and "to prepare their Minds to receive and relish those impressions and sentiments that it is incumbent on us streniously to inculcate upon this Occasion."[53]

The Indians flatly refused to go to Charleston; and Ellis's agent had to enlist the aid of the Indian traders to overcome the reluctance of the chiefs to come even to Savannah. However, on the twenty-fifth of October, 1757, Ellis received word that a large party of Indians had come together on the Altamaha

50. *S. C. Gaz.*, June 21, July 12, 1760; Minutes of Gov. and Council, May 26, 1758, *Col. Records*, VII, 763-65; Ellis to Board of Trade, Mar. 31, 1758, unpub. Col. Records, XXVIII, Part 1, 184-86.

51. Ellis to Lyttelton, May 24, 1757, Lyttelton Papers, Clements Lib.

52. Ellis to Lyttelton, Aug. 25, 1757, *ibid.*

53. Journal of Assembly, July 20, 1757, *Col. Records*, XIII, 226; Minutes of Gov. and Council, June 28, 1757, *ibid.*, VII, 597-98; Ellis to Board of Trade, May 25, 1757, unpub. Col. Records, XXVIII, Part 1, 36-39.

and were on their way to Savannah. This was the signal for Governor Ellis to set in motion the elaborate show designed for the edification and befuddlement of the Creek chiefs. He immediately dispatched Captain Milledge with his troop of Rangers to Fort Argyle on the Ogeechee to escort the party through the last stage of its journey. On the twenty-ninth the troop of Rangers accompanied by about 150 Indians was seen approaching the capital, whereupon, at the Governor's bidding, the principal inhabitants of Savannah got on their horses and went out to meet them in a clearing about a mile from town. The whole entourage, now composed of the gentlemen of the vicinity, followed by the Indians according to their rank, with the Rangers bringing up the rear, halted outside the palisades and were saluted by sixteen cannons mounted for the occasion on several bastions.

At the town gate the horsemen parted and formed two lines, through which the Indians filed into Savannah. Inside, Noble Jones with his militia awaited them. Colonel Jones and his men then led the Indians through the streets of the town. As the procession passed the home of Governor Ellis, the Governor's battery of seven guns saluted them, at which all of the guns on the bluff and on the vessels in the river began booming. A little short of the old filature where the Council and Assembly met, the foot militia moved off to the right and to the left in good order, leaving the Indians facing a company of the Virginia Regiment of Blues drawn up in a line before the state house. The Blues, after firing a volley into the air, smartly lined themselves on either side of the council door. The Indians walked in between to be welcomed in the council chamber by the Governor. After an exchange of greetings, Governor Ellis, hoping that all had been duly impressed, invited the headmen to his house for dinner and gave orders for the lesser chiefs to be shown to the quarters prepared for them.[54]

54. Ellis to Board of Trade, Nov. 25, 1757, unpub. Col. Records, XXVIII, Part 1, 114-17; *S. C. Gaz.*, June 19, 1757; Minutes of Gov. and Council, Oct.

When Governor Ellis and his Council returned to the council chamber on November 3, the Indians were again escorted into the room with great ceremony. The chamber was "thronged with the principal Inhabitants who tended with Anxiety to learn the Events of this Congress upon which the Tranquility of the Province so much depended." After Governor Ellis had read and explained a letter from King George "to his beloved Children of the Creek Nations," which the Indians "relished extremely" and "at every Period declared their Approbation aloud," suitable speeches were made and the presents handed out. When Ellis produced the prepared treaty, "the Council Unanimously approved the Whole of His Honour's Conduct and confessed that more had been effected than there was Reason to expect. . . ."[55]

The treaty signed by Ellis and twenty-one headmen on this occasion was one of friendship and alliance. All former pacts between the colony and the Nation were confirmed, past grievances were buried, and a conventional alliance between Georgia and the Creeks agreed upon. Of particular importance was the specific provision by which both the Governor and the chiefs agreed to accept responsibility for the vagrant misdeeds of any of their people and to mete out the punishment and make the redress that the offense warranted. This provision was included in the subsequent treaties with the Creeks; and, although frequently invoked, neither the whites nor the Indians were ever fully satisfied that the other acted with the dispatch and severity that any particular occasion required.[56]

Governor Ellis was confident that the treaty was the fruit of his talks with his Indian visitors in the spring and summer of 1757. He was especially proud that the Indian chiefs had taken his frequent hints and voluntarily ceded to him the islands of Ossabaw, Sapelo, and St. Catherine's with a formal denial

---

25, 1757, *Col. Records*, VII, 643-48; Ellis to Lyttelton, Nov. 3, 1757, Lyttelton Papers, Clements Lib.

55. Minutes of Gov. and Council, Nov. 3, 1757, *Col. Records*, VII, 657-67.

56. *Ibid.*; Minutes of Gov. and Council, Nov. 7, 1757, *ibid.*, 668.

that they had ever given them to that remarkable Indian woman, Mary Musgrove Bosomworth. Governor Ellis had sensibly refrained from pressing for land concessions inland at this time, but he had been eager to do something about the Bosomworth claims on the coast which for years had been a disruptive factor in the Indian relations of the colony. Nowhere is Ellis's statesmanship more apparent than in his decision not to use the cession to destroy the claims of the troublesome Bosomworths. Instead he strongly urged the Board of Trade to let him make some sort of settlement which would satisfy these people and eliminate the influential Mary as a hostile voice in Indian councils. In the end, the Board agreed; Ellis granted the land on St. Catherine's Island to the Bosomworths and promised them £2000 for the renunciation of all other claims. Georgia thus gained an undisputed title to the three islands while Mary Musgrove Bosomworth, James Oglethorpe's old friend, became a valuable ally in future parleys with the Indians.[57]

For more than two years after the signing of the treaty Ellis had no real trouble with the Creeks. When in 1758 a party of Indians robbed and murdered a family near Savannah, Ellis got the Indians themselves to punish the offenders.[58] He perceived that most of the trouble between the Creeks and the settlers came from the trade of the white men with the Indians, both in frontier settlements and in the Indian villages. Beginning in 1757, he labored to bring the Indian trade under strict control of the government. To prevent irresponsible traders from drawing the colony into hostilities with the Creeks, Governor Ellis and the Assembly ruled that only those with a license from the Governor could trade with the Indians, and then only under certain prescribed conditions. Enforcement was the great difficulty, of course, especially since the Carolina traders in the Creek country were not subject to Ellis's control.

57. Ellis to Board of Trade, Nov. 25, 1757, June 28, 1758, July 26, 1759, unpub. Col. Records, XXVIII, Part 1, 114-17, 220-22, 306-10.
58. Ellis to Board of Trade, Oct. 25, 1758, *ibid.*, 231-33.

Shortly before he left Georgia, Ellis came up with a plan which promised success. Each town of the Creeks was asked to appoint a headman through whom the traders and the colonial government would channel all of their dealings with the Indians. The headman's hand was to be further strengthened by allowing him to store and distribute the English presents in his village. He in turn was to be responsible to the English governor for the good behavior of his people. By restricting the trade to a few licensed traders dealing with only one Indian in a town, Ellis hoped to prevent trouble or, if it should arise, to identify its source immediately.[59]

In 1758 the warriors of the Cherokee Indians returned from Virginia after fighting with the British against the French, highly incensed at the treatment that they had received there from the English. The fear that the Cherokee would join with the Creeks and the two turn upon the settlers of South Carolina and Georgia was momentarily allayed by the news that the Creeks and the Cherokee were themselves on the verge of war. In the summer of 1759, however, the Cherokee made their attack upon the settlers on the South Carolina frontier. A truce secured by Governor Lyttelton in December stopped hostilities for only a short time, and the Cherokee again attacked South Carolina in January 1760. At the outset Governor Ellis had rushed what forces he could muster to the upcountry and "importunately demanded from the Creeks that Assistance which they promised to afford" should the Cherokee attack the whites. He put his carefully hoarded credit for £1000, originally provided for purchasing presents for the Indians, at the disposal of his agents whom he sent into the Indian country to provoke the Creeks into an attack upon the Cherokee. The militia, which Ellis called to arms, remained alerted during the

59. Journal of Assembly, Jan. 11, Feb. 15, 1758, *Col. Records*, XIII, 239, 282; Minutes of Gov. and Council, Dec. 6, 1759, Jan. 31, June 30, 1760, *ibid.*, VIII, 214-15, 226-27, 325-34; Journal of Upper House, Oct. 25, 1759, *ibid.*, XVI, 388; Ellis to Board of Trade, Oct. 25, 1758, July 10, 1760, unpub. Col. Records, XXVIII, Part 1, 231-33, 443-47.

crisis. The Assembly complied with Ellis's request for an appropriation to build several permanent forts, and the town of Savannah was also strongly fortified. Georgia having nearly doubled in size since 1757, Governor Ellis felt that the colonists could now bear the costs of this vital expansion of the defense structure.[60]

During all of this activity the Cherokee continued to leave the people in Georgia unharmed. What did most to restrain the Cherokee, Ellis believed, was their knowledge of the good relations which existed between the rival Creeks and the province of Georgia. Ellis spent the spring of 1760 trying to stir up trouble between the Creeks and Cherokee and "set every Person of Influence upon endeavouring to create a Rupture between those two Nations";[61] but late in May he learned to his dismay that a party of Creeks on the sixteenth had killed several Georgia traders near Augusta—traditionally the equivalent of a declaration of war. Still seeing in a war with the Creeks nothing but an invitation to disaster, Ellis chose to "suffer Justice to give Way to Prudence," as the legislature advised, and sought to avoid war with the Creeks by ostentatiously assuming that the French and not the Creek Nation were responsible for the murders. Ellis went even further to placate the Creeks.[62] He left the apprehension and punishment of the murderers entirely to the Indians, and in July he made a move toward reopening the Creek trade. The presence of nearly two hundred Creeks in the settlements at the time of the outbreak

60. Journal of Upper House, Feb. 12, 1760, *Col. Records*, XVI, 435-36; Minutes of Gov. and Council, Feb. 3, 18, Mar. 26, June 17, 1760, *ibid.*, VIII, 228, 250-51, 266, 324; Ellis to Board of Trade, Nov. 9, 1758, Aug. 25, 1760, unpub. Col. Records, XXVIII, Part 1, 242-43, 456-59; Ellis to Lyttelton, Aug. 27, 1757, ff., Lyttelton Papers, Clements Lib.

61. Journal of Upper House, Feb. 12, 1760, *Col. Records*, XVI, 435; *S. C. Gaz.*, Apr. 12, May 10, 1760; Minutes of Gov. and Council, Feb. 9, 21, Apr. 14, May 2, 20, 1760, *Col. Records*, VIII, 248, 253, 284-85, 295-97, 308-13; Ellis to Board of Trade, Mar. 5, 1760, unpub. Col. Records, XXVIII, Part 1, 341-42.

62. Journal of Upper House, June 2, 1760, *Col. Records*, XVI, 498-99; Ellis to Board of Trade, June 7, 1760, unpub. Col. Records, XXVIII, Part 1, 384-86.

lent weight to Governor Ellis's contention that the murders were not sanctioned by the Nation as a whole; and his forbearance was further justified when an envoy from the Creeks arrived shortly and convinced the whites that the Creek Nation, as such, was not involved.[63]

The great harm done by this incident, to Ellis's thinking, was that it made painfully plain the true weakness of the colony, heretofore "by great Management" partially concealed. Settlers had fled the province by the hundreds, and Ellis's conciliatory policy toward the Creeks under such provocation could only bespeak a weakness which would surely discourage "Persons of real Property" from coming into the colony.[64] In the last letter which he wrote from Georgia a few months later, Ellis gave vent to the bitterness he felt at the British government's neglect of the Georgia frontier:

Meanwhile, I cannot help expressing my surprize that his Majestys Southern Provinces should be suffered so long to continue exposed as they are, considering the vicinity, dispositions, & power of the French, and the Savage Nations connected with them, in this Quarter. Surely my Lords 'tis disgraceful to us that whilst our Arms are every where prevailing over the Forces of the Most formidable state in Europe, a few Tribes of barbarians, are murdering the Kings Subjects, and ravaging his Provinces in America, with impunity. From my soul I wish such inattention may not be productive of the most mischievous consequences.[65]

Despite the bitter note of his valedictory, Governor Ellis had accomplished much. He had succeeded in keeping a firm control over men and events in Georgia. At the end of three years the fruits of his labors were everywhere about him, and they were good. The lower house of the legislature had been kept in line, and all parts of the government were working to-

63. Ellis to Board of Trade, June 7, July 10, 1760, unpub. Col. Records, XXVIII, Part 1, 384-86, 443-47; Minutes of Gov. and Council, May 26, June 5, 1760, *Col. Records*, VIII, 314-17, 319-23.
64. Ellis to Pitt, July 10, 1760, unpub. Col. Records, XXVIII, Part 1, 449-54.
65. Ellis to Board of Trade, Oct. 20, 1760, *ibid.*, 466-70.

gether with unprecedented harmony under his leadership. The colony had been spared the catastrophe of an Indian war largely through his efforts. A respectable defense structure had been built and maintained. The population of the colony was growing steadily for the first time; and its production and trade had more than doubled. He had gained the real affection and respect of the inhabitants and was highly thought of by the Board of Trade. Yet, by the fall of 1759 Ellis had become discouraged and perhaps a little bored. The "intense heats" of the Georgia summers were more than he could bear. Like a suffering David he mourned that the climate had brought him so low that "very little enjoyment of Life" was left him.[66] Even his weekend "House upon the salt water 12 miles out of Town" gave no relief.[67] Whether Henry Ellis in some way lacked ambition, drive, or seriousness of purpose, or whether the malarial attacks did actually incapacitate him, he believed himself ready for retirement. Although a little taken aback by the ready approval of his petition to be relieved of his duties,[68] he set sail from Georgia in early November of 1760, leaving James Wright to act in his stead.

Superficially Henry Ellis and his better known successor were hardly distinguishable. They were both English—one born in Ireland, the other in America, in their middle years, educated, experienced, and wealthy. Both were blessed with the ability, the intelligence, and the character to allow them to become eminently successful colonial governors. But their differences, perhaps no more than a difference of emphasis, make them stand out as contrasting figures in Georgia history. The impression left by these two men on the young colony was in both instances great and good, but good in very dissimilar ways. The two men wholeheartedly subscribed to the contemporary rationale of the British imperial and mercantile

66. Ellis to Board of Trade, Nov. 25, 1759, *ibid.*, 317-18.
67. Ellis to Lyttelton, July 21, 1758, Lyttelton Papers, Clements Lib.
68. Ellis to Lyttelton, Mar. 14, 1760, *ibid.;* Ellis to Amherst, Oct. 5, 1759, ff., Amherst Papers, Lib. Cong.

systems that whatever was good for either Britain or the colonies was good for both. Ellis consistently spoke and acted as if this meant that whatever was to the best interest of Georgia should be adopted in Georgia; the resulting increase in the colony's wealth and power would be the Empire's gain. Wright, on the other hand, tended to believe that the local interests of Georgia had to give way to measures designed for the good of the Empire as a whole. With great devotion and inflexible purpose he undertook to uphold the hand of king and Parliament right up until the day revolution engulfed him, never doubting that the ultimate good of Georgia lay in this direction. Whether the Liberty Boys and the revolutionary mob could have been diverted from their course by Ellis's tact, sympathy, and political stratagems any more than they were in fact intimidated by Wright's unyielding opposition and contemptuous disapproval is a nice question.

CHAPTER IV

Governor James Wright, Unity and Progress, 1760-1765

JAMES WRIGHT, when he took office in the fall of 1760, was to govern Georgia longer than any other man ever has, before or since—twenty-two years in form, fifteen years in fact. He also influenced the course and nature of its development perhaps as much as any other. At the head of the government during the years when the colony enjoyed its first real growth coincident with its involvement in the prolonged constitutional crisis that strained and then cracked the old Empire, he left the definite imprint of his personality upon its character. Wright, whose father had been chief justice of South Carolina, was born in that province but schooled in England. He himself had been attorney general of South Carolina for twenty-one years, but at the time of his appointment as lieutenant governor he was in London acting as agent for his native colony. He soon transferred his considerable property from Carolina across the Savannah River to his new home; and by the time of the Revolution, with an estate valued at more than £80,000, James Wright was undoubtedly the wealthiest man in Georgia.[1]

Wright's ship dropped anchor at Charleston on Sunday afternoon, September 7, 1760. His first unhappy task was to arrange for the burial of his child who had died at sea. Wright

---

1. *S. C. Gaz.*, Mar. 1, 1760; E. Irving Carlyle in *DNB* *s.v.* "Wright, Sir James"; William Bacon Stevens, *A History of Georgia from Its First Discovery by Europeans to the Adoption of the Present Constitution in MDCCXCVIII*, II (Philadelphia, 1859), 18; Memorial of Sir James Wright to Lord George Germain (1777), unpub. Col. Records, XXXIX, 26-29.

and his wife and children visited with friends in Charleston for a month before setting out for Savannah.[2] There he was greeted by Governor Ellis. Ellis, who deferred his departure for several weeks in order to smooth the way for his replacement, reported to the Board of Trade that he was "much pleased" with the new lieutenant governor whom he had found "to be a very capable & worthy man."[3]

The leading men of the colony were likewise pleased. Though regretting the loss of Ellis, they were happy that his replacement was a man of Wright's reputation and stature. In its reply to Wright's opening message to the session of the legislature which convened on November 3, the day after Ellis's departure for New York, the Assembly spoke of Wright's reputation for "Integrity and Uprightness joyned with solid sense and sound Judgment."[4] In these few words, conventionally spoken, they got at the essentials of the man's character. Here are the traits that were to mark his conduct in office for a decade and a half. Not even his most violent political enemies in the seventies—and they were many—could deny him this.

James Wright had little of Henry Ellis's facile cleverness. In the place of Ellis's quick insight into political problems and his flashes of originality in policy, Wright substituted a steady and sound, and growing, understanding of politics gained from long experience in political affairs. Governor Ellis had been able to go to the heart of a matter with remarkable directness and report its gist in incisive and forceful language. Wright, for his part, sometimes confused the inconsequential with the important; his earlier analyses of doings in Georgia were often a little muddled and his reports discursive and repetitious. Ellis had taken the detached, impersonal approach to the art of government, always keeping the desired end in view, while

2. *S. C. Gaz.*, Sept. 13, Oct. 11, 1760.
3. Ellis to Board of Trade, Oct. 20, 1760, unpub. Col. Records, XXVIII, Part 1, 466-70; Wright to Board of Trade, Dec. 23, 1760, *ibid.*, 477-88.
4. Journal of Assembly, Nov. 6, 1760, *Col. Records*, XIII, 439-40; *S. C. Gaz.*, Dec. 23, 1760.

Wright, with his highly developed sense of *amour propre,* was prone to become emotionally involved if he felt that his rightful place in government was challenged or respect due his position withheld. Where Ellis had been adaptable, conciliatory, chameleon-like in his dealings with the colonists, Wright was inclined to be formal and aloof, sometimes stern and, when attacked, unyielding, even arrogant. Instead of depending upon improvisation and clever timing to govern the province, Wright acted from fixed principles of political conduct. In office he was consistent in a time when consistency was sometimes dangerous and not always wise—a man of principle when great principles clashed, a staunch conservative in a time of change, the king's man in a revolution.

The fundamental difference between these two architects of colonial Georgia in 1760 can be got at if it is seen that whereas Henry Ellis had been a young dilettante in politics— astute and gifted certainly, but still basically an amateur and uncommitted—James Wright, a man in his middle years, was from the first a professional, wholly committed, the pattern of his life and character already set. This is not to say that Wright's personality and his ideas did not develop and change under the impact of opposition and eventual rebellion in Georgia, for they did. But the changes came within rather well-defined limits, easily predictable in 1760, and more often than not they tended to strengthen the old pattern rather than to alter it.

It goes without saying that James Wright in Georgia was first and always the servant of the king, an agent of the British government in North America. This is the touchstone of his actions—for Wright and for his historian. Yet he always recognized and fully accepted a definite responsibility to the colony as such. Here again, he had little doubt as to his proper function. Implicit in much of what he wrote about political matters and underlying much of what he did while in office was the conviction that his primary function as governor, in so far as the colony itself was concerned, was to make sure his government served the best interests of those who were in a position to make Georgia productive and prosperous. This could only be done by helping the more able and acquisitive of his charges to accumulate and hold property. In return, Wright expected the propertied people to give his government the material and moral support it needed. As for the "lower classes of people," he believed, the blessings of English law and of English institutions provided reason enough for them to remain loyal: from the courts, they could get justice; under the law, all enjoyed more liberty than most were fit to exercise. Besides, could not the Cracker become a planter simply by summoning the energy and initiative to make use of the land and credit available to him? Since the interests of the mother country and of the colonists were both best served by a prosperous and productive colony, Governor Wright was inclined to lay the blame for any ambiguity in his position, for any conflict of interests between his two responsibilities, either upon the unwise policy of the British government or, more often, upon the willful and shortsighted obstructionism of the colonists.

The partnership of government with mercantile and agricultural interests was, of course, a commonplace of mid-eighteenth-century British politics. Both Ellis and Reynolds had taken it for granted. Wright, for his part, not only accepted it, but he believed, almost passionately, that the British Empire had developed by the 1760's a series of political and economic relationships not perfect perhaps but so good that only fools would tamper with them to correct supposed faults, at worst minor or transitory, lest the whole delicate balance be upset. Furthermore, conditions permitted Wright to use the resources of government in support of business in a way that had been impossible for his predecessors. In the first few years of Wright's administration, an easing of tension in Indian affairs allowed his government to give the merchant and planter an open field for expansion as well as tangible aid. Heretofore, the most the governor had even hoped to do was give the settlers a modicum of security from Indian attack, provide them with land and a little credit perhaps, and maintain at least a minimum of order and respect for law.

As the new governor moved easily into Ellis's place, the colonists were relieved to learn that there was going to be no radical change in policy.[5] Wright, who saw Georgia's problems in much the same light as Ellis, undertook to carry on the projects and policies already begun by his predecessor. Even so, almost at once the force of Wright's personality made itself felt in the colony. In public affairs there was a subtle shift of emphasis, a slackening off, a slowing of the pace. Gone was the sense of urgency, of moving from crisis to crisis, each demanding every bit of ingenuity and all of the resources at the colony's disposal. Life, if less exciting, became less harrowing. The Assembly was soon able to forget the Indians long enough to worry about digging wells and building a jail, and even the need of doing something for the encouragement of virtue and punishment of vice on this rough frontier. At times in the past almost overpowered by the rush of events and by Ellis's irresistible supervision of its transactions, the Assembly under Wright developed new independence and dignity. While continuing the governor's active participation in legislative affairs, Wright depended less upon tact and charm and more upon treating the assemblymen as sensible men politically mature enough to assume responsibility for working with the governor for their own good and for the good of the province. Instead of specific instructions with drafts of proposed bills, the legislature usually got from Wright only a survey of the situation with general suggestions for legislation. As long as the Governor and the legislature remained in basic agreement on policy, the Assembly responded admirably to this light rein.

When Governor Ellis turned the government over to Wright in November, though confident that he was leaving the

5. *S. C. Gaz.*, Nov. 29, 1760, Feb. 7, 1761.

province "in full as good a situation, as could reasonably be expected," he cautioned that the colony was "still on a very ticklish footing" with the Creeks, despite the steps he had taken to restore the good relations strained to the breaking point in May by the murder of the traders.[6] Concurring with Ellis's policy of conciliation, Wright was as firmly persuaded that a Creek war was to be avoided at all costs. He fully approved of Ellis's decision not to await his arrival before inviting the Creek headmen to Savannah. After the Indians began to come into town in early November, hardly a week went by during the next six or eight months without Wright having a talk with one group of Creeks or another. The party's spokesmen vehemently denied that the Creek Nation had had anything to do with the attack on the traders. They insisted instead that the deed was done without the Nation's knowledge by a few hotheaded young warriors. Betraying what mainly had drawn them to Savannah, they urged the full resumption of trade in the Indian country. A number slyly suggested that the arguments of the French and Cherokee designed to draw the Creeks into the war against the English were made much stronger by the scarcity of English goods in their towns.

Governor Wright made no attempt to match wits with "the wretches." Nor did he try to win them over by the use of flattery and elaborate diplomacy. He was satisfied to bid for their respect by treating them with what he considered fairness. For the rest, he relied only upon self-interest and the fear of retribution to carry weight with the Indians. Although sternly reminding the visiting Creeks that they were obliged by treaty to assume responsibility for the murders whether they had sanctioned them or not, Wright stopped short of an outright demand for satisfaction. By describing the deplorable state of the Cherokee who had dared to attack South Carolina and by telling them of British victories over the French in the North,

6. Ellis to Board of Trade, Oct. 20, 1760, unpub. Col. Records, XXVIII, Part 1, 466-70.

he sought to leave the impression that for the Creeks to lean upon these two broken reeds would only be to invite a like fate.[7]

In the spring of 1761 the upcountry was rapidly recovering from the setback caused by the flight of the settlers at the threat of a Creek war. In his message to the General Assembly in March, Governor Wright was cautiously optimistic about the prospects of peace on the Indian front. This was excuse enough for the House of Assembly to cut expenditures for defense, which had been a constant and heavy drain since the start of the French war, by voting to suspend work on the fortifications begun by Ellis at Savannah.[8] When a gang of Creeks in June murdered a settler on the northern frontier, far from throwing Governor Wright into a panic, the incident gave him a psychological advantage which he was quick to take advantage of. After hearing the Creeks talk for nine months of their love for the English and of their intention to punish any of their people who should jeopardize the good relations between the Indians and whites, Wright could now afford to ignore the claims of the Creek envoys who came to Savannah in August that the killing grew out of a private quarrel in which the white man was at fault, as was probably the case.[9]

During these negotiations with the Indians, Governor Wright became confirmed in his opinion that most of the colony's trouble with them could be traced to the trade carried on in the Creek country by the white traders, that "very worst & most abandoned Set of Men." In the summer of 1761, when the Creek towns were again being visited by the traders returning after their flight a year before, Wright "found the Indian Trade Running into Great Confusion." If the traders

7. Minutes of Gov. and Council, Nov. 7-21, 1760, Jan. 29, Mar. 4, 31, July 28, 1761, *Col. Records*, VIII, 414-33, 469-70, 512, 520-21, 540-46; *S. C. Gaz.*, Nov. 29, Dec. 16, 1760, Feb. 7, 1761; Wright to Board of Trade, May 26, Feb. 4, 1764, unpub. Col. Records, XXVIII, Part 2, 60-67, 16-21.

8. *The London Chronicle: or, Universal Evening Post*, Aug. 19, 1760; *S. C. Gaz.*, June 10, 1760; Journal of Assembly, Mar. 25, May 21, 1761, *Col. Records*, XIII, 474-76, 568.

9. Minutes of Gov. and Council, Aug. 4, 1761, *Col. Records*, VIII, 553-57.

were not cheating the Indians, they were busy persuading them that their competitors were. There were "Continual Complaints" from both. For Wright, not the least disadvantage of this unfettered free enterprise was that the Indians were being oversupplied with goods. On the theory that one of the strongest curbs on their tendency to mischief was their yen for English goods, Wright maintained that good policy required that the Indians never be given so much that they did not fear the stoppage of the trade and never so little as to make them desperate.[10]

The importance Wright attached to the Indian trade led him to attempt to devise a more satisfactory way of exchanging English goods for the skins of the deer and beaver trapped by the Indians. His plan, instituted in the summer of 1761, abandoned Ellis's hopeful scheme for developing a responsible Indian in each of the Creek towns. Wright concentrated on the traders instead. He chose a dozen or so individuals or firms to handle the entire commerce with both the Upper and the Lower Creeks. To each he gave a license authorizing him to handle all the trade in certain towns. In this way, the trade was restricted to a manageable number of men. These regulations remained in force until the summer of 1764 when the Board of Trade required the governor to resume giving all comers permission to trade wherever they pleased. Wright insisted, and continued to insist, that free trade with the Indians was entirely unsuited to local conditions—but to no avail.[11]

In the summer of 1761 the traders still had not returned to their towns in the numbers desired by the Creeks. Fearful of further tightening of the trade, the Indians behaved so well to Wright that by November of 1761 he could tell the Assembly

10. Wright to Board of Trade, Aug. 27, 1764, unpub. Col. Records, XXVIII, Part 2, 114-16; Minutes of Gov. and Council, Mar. 10, Dec. 15, 1761, Feb. 19, July 6, Oct. 5, 1762, *Col. Records,* VIII, 514-15, 617, 649, 708, 756.

11. Minutes of Gov. and Council, July 3, 1761, Aug. 7, 1764, *Col. Records,* VIII, 522-24, IX, 202; Wright to Board of Trade, Aug. 27, Dec. 11, 1764, Aug. 19, 1765, June 28, 1766, unpub. Col. Records, XXVIII, Part 2, 114-16, 158-59, 250-51, 361-62.

that the Creeks at last appeared "disposed to Continue in Friendship" with the colony. This development, combined with reports of the Cherokee's intention to make peace with South Carolina, encouraged Wright to suggest that the legislature divert a part of the public money from defense of the frontier to the building of a fort on the lower Savannah for the promotion of trade, from the first a great object with the Governor and the legislature.[12]

The need for a fort at the mouth of the Savannah had been brought forcibly to Wright's attention several months before when a privateer in July had sent a landing party ashore at Tybee, an island on the coast down the river from Savannah, and sailed off with a number of Negroes. After sending a scout boat in pursuit and stationing a watch on the island, Wright called on the engineer John Gerar William De Brahm to draw up a sketch of a battery of six guns to be built on Cockspur Island between Tybee and the town. The Council approved Wright's proposal to begin work on the battery immediately; and when the legislature met in the fall, the Assembly granted his request for authority to construct a full-sized fort on Cockspur. Rumors that Spain was coming into the war on the side of the French prompted the governor to send in the spring of 1762 a detachment of Rangers down to Cockspur for the purpose of protecting the men working on the fort. With Spanish ships both at Havana and at St. Augustine, the news of the actual outbreak of hostilities, received at Savannah on May 25, 1762, made the new fort, called Fort George, seem vitally important. As it turned out, Georgia's part in the Spanish war consisted largely of attempts by officials to deter the citizenry from trading with the Spanish in Florida.[13]

When word came to Savannah in the spring of 1763 that the Treaty of Paris had been signed and that France and Spain were withdrawing from this part of the New World, a general

12. Journal of Assembly, Nov. 11, 1761, *Col. Records*, XIII, 587.
13. Minutes of Gov. and Council, July 28, 1761, Apr. 22, May 25, 27, 1762, *ibid.*, VIII, 540-41, 673, 687-88, 688-90; *S. C. Gaz.*, May 15, 29, June 12, 1762.

settlement with the southern Indians became urgent. The day for Georgia and Carolina to put the Indians permanently on the defensive had at last arrived. Orders from the Earl of Egremont came to Wright about the first of June instructing him to join with Captain John Stuart, superintendent of Indian affairs for the southern district, and the governors of the other southern colonies in calling a general Indian congress. Wright was fearful that the feelings of the Indians toward the British were not at the moment "the most cordial & friendly."[14] He knew them to be alarmed at the French and Spanish leaving the English a free hand in this part of the world. The anxiety of the southern tribes over the constant push of the English to the westward was apparent. The Creeks of Georgia had shown their resentment of the "Virginia People," who they said were moving in on their land in increasing numbers.[15] Governor Wright, however, strongly favored the congress and, despite his misgivings, believed that it would be a success.

Several months passed before a time and place for the meeting could be agreed upon, presents accumulated, and the Indians invited. It was well into October before the Indians began to converge on Augusta to exchange talks with the governors. Setting out from Savannah on October 20, Wright was ceremoniously escorted up to Augusta, and got there on the twenty-fifth in time to witness the late arrival of the other governors, Arthur Dobbs, Thomas Boone, and Francis Fauquier, who had been loath to leave the comforts of Charleston for the uncertain accommodations of rude Augusta. Their last-minute attempt to move the conference to Dorchester near Charleston, bitterly opposed by Wright, had been thwarted by the Indians' refusal to go a step farther than Augusta. Governor Wright opened the conference on Saturday, November

14. Wright to Egremont, June 10, 1763, unpub. Col. Records, XXXVII, 50-53. As early as 1761, the Board of Trade had offered Wright an extra supply of presents whenever he should think the time ripe for bargaining with the Indians.

15. Minutes of Gov. and Council, July 14, 1763, *Col. Records*, IX, 70-79.

5, to an assemblage of some seven or eight hundred Chicasaw, Choctaw, Cherokee, Catawba, and Creeks. After three days of talk, the Indians and governors signed the treaty reaffirming their pledges of friendship; and, in return for forgiveness of their past sins, the Creeks ceded to Georgia a sizable tract of land.[16]

The congress indirectly had one unfortunate consequence. As so often happened after a major concession to the whites, the irreconcilables among the tribesmen struck back blindly. On New Year's Day, 1764, a party of young Creeks murdered fourteen people at Long Cane settlement in the South Carolina upcountry. In the end, the Creeks satisfied Governor Boone's demands for restitution and confirmed the cessions without further protest.[17] Then a great quiet seemed to descend on the Creek Nation. For the first time since white men had come across the Savannah River to live, the danger of Indian attack receded, at least for the moment, into the realm of the unlikely. James Habersham wrote to England that the colonists appeared to be in no more apprehension of Indian attack than the people of London.[18] After many years of teetering on the brink of destruction, Georgia was never again to have any real doubts as to who should win in a war with the Indians. The Indians could, and did, give Georgia trouble for another fifty years and more; but, stripped of their allies and faced with an ever-increasing horde of white settlers, they could not threaten its survival.

16. Minutes of Gov. and Council, Oct. 11, 1763, *ibid.*, 97-99; Wright to Egremont, June 10, 1763, unpub. Col. Records, XXXVII, 50-53; Lt. Gov. Fauquier to Wright, May 27, 1763, *ibid.*, 56; Wright to Fauquier, June 22, 1763, *ibid.*, 57-60; Ga. Gaz., Oct. 27, Nov. 3, 10, 1763; *Journal of the Congress of the Four Southern Governors, and the Superintendent of that District, with the Five Nations of Indians, at Augusta, 1763* (Charleston, 1764).

17. S. C. Gaz., Jan. 14, 1764, ff.; Minutes of Gov. and Council, Jan. 16, 1764, *Col. Records*, IX, 111-17; Wright to Board of Trade, Jan. 17, Feb. 4, May 26, Aug. 27, Dec. 14, 1764, unpub. Col. Records, XXVIII, Part 2, 2-4, 16-21, 60-67, 114-16, 161-63.

18. Habersham to William Russell, Oct. 10, 1764, Ga. Hist. Soc., *Colls.*, VI, 26-27.

Although neither Governor Wright nor the colonists at first realized its full implications, the establishment of English control in East and West Florida had in fact revolutionized the entire situation in Georgia.[19]   Security and defense were no longer to be the prime object of the colony and its government. They could now turn their full attention to production and trade.   Where Georgia had before been a buffer state, a shaky military outpost, it was now free to become a productive unit in the commercial system of the Empire.   A clear path to wealth and power seemed to lie before the colony.

As a matter of fact, as early as 1761 there had been discernible in the House of Assembly a decided shift from preoccupation with defense to measures for the promotion of trade.   The death of George II caused Governor Wright to call for new elections in the early spring of that year.   For nearly four years, until it was dissolved at its own request in September 1764, this Assembly worked in close cooperation with the Governor primarily for the promotion of trade.   To facilitate navigation, it took steps to clear the streams, to keep up the lighthouse at Tybee Island, and to hire pilots for the harbors of Sunbury and Savannah.[20]   So that the export trade would not suffer from the shipping of inferior products, the Assembly initiated requirements for the inspection of pork, beef, rice, indigo, and lumber products.[21]   Certain taxes were designed to encourage local cultivation and to increase the shipping from the two

19. Committee of Correspondence to William Knox, Mar. 13, 1764, *ibid.*, 18-19; Wright to Board of Trade, Mar. 27, 1764, unpub. Col. Records, XXVIII, Part 2, 41-43.

20. *An Act to prevent persons throwing Ballast or Rubbish or falling Trees into the Rivers and navigable Creeks within this Province, and for keeping Clear the Channels of the same; An Act for Raising and granting to his Majesty the Sum of One Hundred and Eighty Pounds to Repair the Light House on Tybee Island and for laying a Duty on Negroes that have been above Six Months in any of the Islands or Colonies in America and Imported for Sale into this Province; An Act for raising and granting to his Majesty the Sum of one hundred and ninety three Pounds ten shillings for applying the same towards the better support and Encouragement of the Pilots for the service of the Province. . . .*

21. When an inspection bill was finally passed by the legislature, January 21, 1766, rice and indigo were omitted.

ports of the colony.[22]   A bill laying a tax on deerskins sent to
Charleston from Augusta was assented to by Governor Wright,
without the Board of Trade's prior consent, mainly for the
purpose of diverting a greater volume of the fur trade from
Charleston to Savannah.[23]   The proceeds of the tax went to
build Fort George on Cockspur, which gave protection to shipping in the river and allowed Governor Wright to enforce the
laws of trade.   For the first time, the legislature sent an agent
to London to watch over the interests of the colony and of its
merchants and planters in particular.   To correspond with him,
it set up a joint committee of both houses to be called the committee of correspondence.[24]   The legislature with the support of
Governor Wright also got permission from London in 1761 to
make another issue of paper money, which was vital to further
commercial expansion.[25]

This legislation in part reflected and in part stimulated the
growth of the colony and its increased economic activity in these
three or four years.   The prosperity begun under Ellis had
continued unchecked into Wright's administration.   For several
years the annual increase in exports was on an average roughly
equivalent to its whole value in 1759.[26]   Savannah, heretofore
little more than an extension of the port at Charleston, began
to develop as a port in its own right, and soon had ships going
to and from Britain.   The fur trade, long a virtual monopoly
of the Charleston merchants, began to be an important factor
in the Georgia economy as the skins found their way down the
river and onto the waiting ships along with the rapidly in-

22. *An Act to oblige Masters of Vessels Super-Cargoes and other transient
Persons importing Goods and Merchandize into this Province to pay Tax for the
same.*
23. Journal of Assembly, Dec. 2, 1761, *Col. Records*, XIII, 616-19; Wright
to Board of Trade, Feb. 20, 1762, unpub. Col. Records, XXVIII, Part 1, 600-5.
24. Journal of Assembly, Dec. 14, 1761, *Col. Records*, XIII, 628; *S. C. Gaz.*,
Feb. 20, 1762.
25. Journal of Assembly, Apr. 10, 13-14, 1761, *Col. Records*, XIII, 506-7,
509-12; Wright to Board of Trade, Apr. 15, 1761, unpub. Col. Records, XXVIII,
Part 1, 511-16.
26. De Brahm, *History of Georgia*, 51-53.

creasing produce from the plantations.[27] In 1764, the year that
the Assembly was dissolved, the exports of the colony were
nearly equal both in volume and in value to the combined total
of the four-year period, 1756-60.[28] And this was only the
beginning.

Even though the House of Assembly from the start worked
in close harmony with Governor Wright for the promotion of
trade and the regulation of Indian affairs, it early found opportunity to test the new Governor's mettle. When the Governor sent his first annual estimate of current expenses to the
House in March 1761, Chief Justice William Grover was
summoned (at the suggestion of one of the members) to testify
as to the propriety of the colony paying the usual supplement
to the crown officials' salaries. Grover testified that when
offering him the justiceship Lord Halifax had said that crown
officers could expect no fees from the public in Georgia. On
the strength of this, the Assembly struck several items from
Wright's estimate.[29]

Uncertain of his ground, Governor Wright was slow in
responding. While awaiting instructions from the Board of
Trade, he continued to pay all of the officials except Grover,
who refused the six pounds usually paid the chief justice.[30]
When the legislature next convened in November 1761, the
salary supplement issue was avoided, but there was an under-
current of tension.[31] Wright asked the Board of Trade not
to elevate Lewis Johnson and John Graham, leaders of the
Assembly, to the Council as he had previously requested, lest
their removal from the lower house put him *"to some* difficulty"

27. Journal of Assembly, Dec. 2, 1761, *Col. Records,* XIII, 617; Wright to
Board of Trade, Feb. 20, 1762, unpub. Col. Records, XXVIII, Part 1, 600-5;
Ga. Gaz., Apr. 7, 1763, ff.
28. De Brahm, *History of Georgia,* 52.
29. Journal of Assembly, Apr. 14, May 15, 1761, Oct. 26, 1762, *Col. Records,*
XIII, 512-16, 559-60, 703-5; Wright to Board of Trade, July 13, 1761, unpub.
Col. Records, XXVIII, Part 1, 561-68.
30. William Clifton's affidavit, unpub. Col. Records, XXVIII, Part 1, 579;
Wright to Board of Trade, July 13, 1761, *ibid.,* 561-68.
31. Journal of Assembly, Nov. 30, 1761, Feb. 25, 1762, *Col. Records,* XIII,
610, 686; Journal of Upper House, Feb. 26, 1762, *ibid.,* XVI, 685.

there.[32] Not until the third session of the legislature, which
opened in October 1762, was Wright finally ready to meet the
issue squarely. Armed with a letter from the Board of Trade
approving his estimate and critical of Grover's testimony, the
Governor sent down to the House the identical estimate for
the supplement to the salaries of crown officers that he had submitted in March of the preceding year.[33] No objection was
offered in the House. By this time the complexion of things
had completely changed. Open warfare between the Governor
and the chief justice was now raging, and the House of Assembly was poised to enter the fray on the side of the Governor.

William Grover, chief justice of Georgia since 1759 and its
first, had quit attending the meetings of the Council several
months before Wright's arrival because of some differences with
Governor Ellis after having become involved in a public scandal
with Mrs. Clifton, the wife of the attorney general.[34] He
continued to stay away even after Ellis's departure, and
Wright's letter of February 12, 1761, requiring his attendance
provoked his resignation from the Council, which Wright persuaded him to withdraw. Grover's testimony before the Assembly a few days later irritated the Governor and he soon
found reason to be displeased with his conduct on the bench.
In July the Governor set aside one of Grover's court orders,
and then in October he made some changes in court procedure
and instructed the chief justice to submit a report on all those
sentenced in his court. At this, Grover resigned from the Council for good. Then, from the fall of 1761 until September of the
next year, the chief justice worked in open opposition to the
Governor. Wright continued to disapprove of many of the
chief justice's decisions and came to believe that the judge was
guilty of actual misconduct in office.[35] When Wright submitted

32. Feb. 20, 1762, unpub. Col. Records, XXVIII, Part 1, 600-5.
33. Journal of Assembly, Oct. 26, 1762, *Col. Records,* XIII, 703-5.
34. Minutes of Gov. and Council, Apr. 9, 1759, *ibid.,* VIII, 27; Ellis to
Lyttelton, June 6, Sept. 8, 1759, Lyttelton Papers, Clements Lib.
35. Wright to Board of Trade, Dec. 28, 1761, June 10, Nov. 8, 1762, unpub.
Col. Records, XXVIII, Part 1, 592-95, 635-40, 670-81; Wright to Egremont,

the evidence against Grover to the Council on September 21, 1762, the councilors were "unanimous and clear in Opinion" that Grover's conduct as chief justice had been "dishonourable, partial, arbitrary, illegal, indecent, and not consistent with the Character, Duty, and Dignity of his Office."[36] After the Council reaffirmed its opinion on October 5, Wright ordered Grover's suspension from office as of November 5, 1762.[37]

A few days after the chief justice's suspension took effect, something happened to bring the House of Assembly openly to the support of the Governor in his feud with the unpopular Grover. On November 17, a doggerel[38] was "found Inscribed on the Wall of An Apartment near the State House,"[39] which the Assembly a few days later censured "as a scandalous and malicious Libel," highly inflammatory and grossly insulting to the Governor and to both houses of the legislature.[40] For a time "it was generally suspected"[41] that Henry Kennan, a member of the Assembly and a friend of Grover's,[42] was the culprit; but on December 9 he made a formal denial satisfactory to the House.[43] When the investigation was dropped the next day with an apology to the Governor from both houses, Wright made it plain that there was no doubt in anyone's mind but that the real author of the piece was Grover himself.[44]

The end result of the Grover affair was to bring the legisla-

---

Jan. 3, 1763, *ibid.*, XXXVII, 18-28; Minutes of Gov. and Council, Feb. 12, July 13, Oct. 6, 1761, Sept. 21, 1762, *Col. Records*, VIII, 497, 530-38, 579-81, 735-49.

36. Minutes of Gov. and Council, Sept. 21, 1762, *Col. Records*, VIII, 736.
37. *Ibid.*, 751; unpub. Col. Records, XXXVII, 33-34.
38. For a copy of the "Libel" see unpub. Col. Records, XXVIII, Part 1, 700.
39. Journal of Assembly, Dec. 10, 1762, *Col. Records*, XIII, 753.
40. Journal of Assembly, Nov. 23, 1762, *ibid.*, 733.
41. Journal of Assembly, Nov. 26, 1762, *ibid.*, 741.
42. Bonds, Bills of Sale, Deeds of Gift, Powers of Attorney: 1765, September 5-1772, Mar. 5, Georgia Department of Archives and History, Atlanta. Item dated July 15, 1766.
43. Journal of Assembly, Nov. 30, Dec. 9, 1762, *Col. Records*, XIII, 743-44, 750-51.
44. Journal of Assembly, Dec. 10, 1762, *ibid.*, 753; Postscript dated Dec. 10, 1762, Wright to Board of Trade, Nov. 8, 1762, unpub. Col. Records, XXVIII, Part 1, 670-81; Wright to Robert Wood, Nov. 15, 1762, *ibid.*, XXXVII, 15-17.

ture and the Governor into even closer union, and for three years there was never the least sign of disagreement or ill feeling. The union between the two was further cemented at the war's end by their mutual chagrin at the prospect that some of the choice fruits of victory would be snatched from them by neighboring South Carolina. Hardly had Charleston gotten news of the provisional treaty with France and Spain in 1763 than Governor Thomas Boone made it known he would accept applications for grants of land between the Altamaha River in Georgia and the St. Johns in Florida, an area formerly claimed by both Britain and Spain. When Governor Wright informed the Assembly on March 25 of Boone's intentions, the two houses prepared to instruct William Knox, the colonial agent in London, to spare no pains or expense to secure disapproval of Boone's steps.[45] Councilor Grey Elliott left for Charleston with Governor Wright's protest and caveat against Boone's assuming jurisdiction over these lands to the south of Savannah. On April 5, Governor Boone, having refused to accept the caveat and having ordered the colonial secretary not to record it, immediately issued warrants of survey for 343,000 of the upwards of 400,000 acres of Altamaha lands applied for that day. Speculation fever had hit Charleston. During the next day or two the mad rush of applicants and surveyors past Savannah by land and by sea began. Although Boone gave out additional warrants on subsequent land days, only fifty-six grants comprising approximately 90,000 acres had actually been registered when instructions from the Board of Trade put a stop to the whole proceedings in the early summer.

Governor Boone based South Carolina's claim to the Altamaha lands on the fact that this area was not included in Georgia's charter and consequently was presumably still a part of South Carolina, from which Georgia had been carved. Governor Wright opposed this claim with arguments both legal

45. Journal of Assembly, Mar. 25, 28, 1763, *Col. Records*, XIV, 59, 61; Journal of Upper House, Mar. 25, 28, 1763, *ibid.*, XVII, 48-52.

and historical, but he talked mostly of the unhappy consequences and the plain injustice of allowing Boone's friends to
monopolize the land. The engrossment of the best part of the
land by only a few men who would never cultivate it, Wright
argued, would shut off from the colony the ready flow of
settlers, "the Sinews, Wealth and Strength of an Infant
Colony."[46] Furthermore it seemed hard that the people of
Georgia who had "borne the brunt & fatigue of settling a new
Colony" and had "encounter'd and struggled with innumerable
difficulties & hardships," and were just now in a way to prosper,
should see the land "swallowed up by Strangers" and themselves "not to have an inch" of it.[47]

Recognizing the merits of Wright's argument, the Board of
Trade assured him that the Altamaha lands would be annexed
to his government and promised it would seek legal means "to
set aside the Grants unwarrantably made" by Governor Boone.[48]
Wright got this good news early in 1764, but later in the year
the Board shifted responsibility back to him. In a letter dated
July 12, 1764, Governor Wright was told to find some way
either to invalidate Boone's grants or to oblige the grantees
to cultivate their claims. The Board of Trade promised to
concur "in any reasonable law" which the legislature might
frame for this purpose.[49] In April 1765, the Governor sent to
England an act requiring the South Carolina claimants to settle
their land with whites and slaves in proportion to the acreage
of their grants. The act was considered discriminatory in
London and was disallowed.[50] All subsequent efforts to oust

46. Wright to Board of Trade, Apr. 20, May 6, June 3, 22, Dec. 23, 1763,
unpub. Col. Records, XXVIII, Part 1, 730-38, 763-65, 767-71, 795-96, 813-15;
July 5, 1764, *ibid.*, XXVIII, Part 2, 81-84; Wright to Egremont, Apr. 20, May
6, Dec. 23, 1763, *ibid.*, XXXVII, 36-45, 47-50, 69-71; Ga. Hist. Soc., *Colls.*,
VI, 10-15; S. C. *Gaz.*, Apr. 9, 1763; Ga. *Gaz.*, Apr. 21, 1763; Minutes of Gov.
and Council, Mar. 28, 1763, *Col. Records*, IX, 51.
47. Wright to Egremont, Apr. 20, 1763, unpub. Col. Records, XXXVII,
36-45.
48. Board of Trade to Wright, Sept. 30, 1763, *ibid.*, XXXIV, 533-35.
49. Board of Trade to Wright, July 12, 1764, *ibid.*, 548-50.
50. Wright to Board of Trade, Apr. 4, 1765, *ibid.*, XXVIII, Part 2, 180-85;
Journal of Assembly, Mar. 25, 1765, *Col. Records*, XIV, 253.

the South Carolinians failed, and they were still in technical possession when the Revolution began. The truth of the matter is that Boone's grants turned out to be not nearly so important as Wright had at first supposed. He had greatly overestimated the demand for land in this region. Even a decade after the Revolution, only a handful of people were living south of the Altamaha.

The leading men of the colony came to have so much confidence in the Governor that the Assembly elected in 1761 did little more in its fourth and last session during the winter of 1763-64 than to pass the annual tax bill, leaving Wright a free hand to deal with the Long Cane outbreak and the Altamaha lands controversy.[51] The next winter the new House of Assembly was kept busy adapting the laws of the colony to its growing size and wealth. Smallpox having broken out in Savannah in the spring of 1764, the only burning issue of the day was whether to inoculate or not to inoculate.[52] On every occasion, both Governor Wright and the House of Assembly congratulated themselves on the "great Unanimity" and the "general Harmony" which subsisted between them, as if they themselves found it incredible. Out of this unanimity and harmony suddenly erupted the violent passion and bitter animosity of the Stamp Act days. The love feast was finished in 1765, never to be resumed.

51. The General Assembly was called into a short session, May 26 to May 29, 1764, to pass a bill for giving aid to the inhabitants of Savannah, who were suffering from a smallpox epidemic.
52. *Ga. Gaz.*, May 31, 1764, ff.

CHAPTER V

Governor Wright and the Stamp Act Tumults, 1765-1766

WHILE TRAVELING in Georgia in September 1765, John Bartram recorded in his diary that James Wright "is universaly respected by all the inhabitants they can hardly say enough in his praise."[1] Five months later some of these same inhabitants were publicly advocating shooting him. This altered feeling toward Wright arose out of the controversy over the Stamp Act. Not that the actual operation of the tax for a few short months had a drastic effect. On the contrary, when the other American ports were closed during the winter, Savannah buzzed with unprecedented activity.

What threatened to turn provincial politics upside down, and did in fact alter the pattern of political relationships in colonial Georgia, was the widespread defiance of the law set at odds with Governor Wright's fixed determination to carry it out to the last letter. Above all else, it was Wright's success in enforcing the law, particularly in the face of the failure of the other royal governors, that did the damage. He showed himself to be an agent, and an extremely effective one, of the British government, who had found his duty in sacrificing the obvious interests of the colony at the bidding of his masters at Whitehall. No longer could he be universally looked upon with friendly respect as the unchallenged leader of the colony. His devotion and his success in upholding the king's part de-

1. John Bartram, *Diary of a Journey Through the Carolinas, Georgia and Florida: From July 1, 1765, to April 10, 1766* (Philadelphia, 1942), 29.

manded and won for him grudging respect and admiration, but no man who was a colonist first, and only secondly a loyal servant of the king, could ever again give James Wright his unreserved support and trust.

The first official reaction in Georgia to the information that Parliament intended to impose a stamp duty in America was a letter from the committee of correspondence to the colonial agent, William Knox, written April 15, 1765.[2] While acknowledging that the tax might be "as equal as any, that could be generally imposed on the Colonys," the committee objected to it as a dangerous precedent. The necessary provincial taxes alone it considered as heavy a burden as the colony could bear. Knox was told to join with the other agents in opposing the tax, but was warned to be discreet. The warning was hardly necessary. In July Governor Wright got a printed copy of a letter written by Knox aggressively defending Parliament's right to levy the tax, a letter that was to have the most serious consequences when its contents became generally known in the colony. (The motives for his zealous advocacy of the Stamp Act, even though an agent for two American colonies, became suspect when a short time later he was made an undersecretary of state for trade and plantations.) Knox, who had been a rice planter in Georgia for several years before his return to London in 1762, was a close friend both of James Habersham, president of the Council, and of Governor Wright. At Habersham's insistence, Wright suppressed the letter and for a time its contents remained unknown in Georgia. For this reason, Knox's failure to align himself with the other agents against the tax was at first looked upon by the more conservative Georgians not as a betrayal but as the mark of superior wisdom and restraint. By the time the legislature convened in October, however, Knox's stand on the Stamp Act was completely understood and universally disliked.[3]

2. Ga. Hist. Soc., *Colls.*, VI, 33.
3. Habersham to Knox, July 17, 18, Oct. 28, 30, 1765, *ibid.*, 38-40, 40-41, 44-46, 46-49.

All during the summer and early fall, letters and papers from the other colonies poured into Georgia, spreading the rising fever of opposition.[4]   Just one week before the Stamp Act was due to go into effect, the "mob" made its first appearance in Savannah.   Presaging the days a decade later when it would overthrow royal government, the mob grew in size and violence with each successive appearance until the Governor finally restored order.   The demonstrations in October were comparatively mild and innocent.   The first took place on a Friday, October 25, the anniversary of George III's accession. The usual ceremonies, including a general muster of the militia, brought many people into the town during the day.   At dusk, a growing crowd began to follow the effigy of a stamp officer being paraded through the streets.   The climax of the evening came when the effigy was "hanged and burnt, amidst the acclamations of a great concourse of people of all ranks and denominations."[5]

The celebration of the anniversary of the Gunpowder Plot on the next Tuesday provided the occasion for the second anti-Stamp Act demonstration.   As was the custom, sailors from the ships that happened to be in the river took part in the parade, and several of the seamen decided to liven up the proceedings a bit.   Six of them showed up in town supporting a scaffold.   On the scaffold stood one of their shipmates who impersonated the "Stamp-master" by holding a paper in his hand while a rope was looped around his neck.   From time to time the sailors set their burden down and, when a crowd had gathered, began to beat their friend with a cudgel.   With every blow, the sailor on the scaffold would bleat out, *"No Stamps, No riot act, Gentlemen, etc."*   After abusing him around the town with other indignities congenial to a sailor's mind, they hauled the scaffold off to Machenry's tavern.   There, before a large gathering, they actually strung the poor fellow up, first

4. Wright to Board of Trade, Nov. 9, 1765, unpub. Col. Records, XXVIII, Part 2, 292-93.
5. *Ga. Gaz.*, Oct. 31, 1765.

having tied a rope under his arms. Through it all, the crowd was "highly diverted with the humour of the tars."[6]

While the citizenry in general was having its fun with the dummies and sailors, there were some who were giving serious thought to what should be done about the Stamp Act, due to begin operation on November 1. Apparently the colonial leaders were united in opinion that the imposition of such a tax by a legislature not elected by them and ignorant of local conditions was a serious infringement on their rights as Englishmen. Certainly they were all alarmed lest the sale of the stamped paper drain off the specie of the colony, bringing economic ruin: in late October, there was an exaggerated notion, almost a feeling of panic, about the probable effect of the tax. Where the division came among the colonists, and it became more marked as time went by, was in how best to oppose the act. President Habersham, the Council, and many of the merchants favored working for repeal in the accepted fashion, through remonstrance and petition.[7] Others more radical, inspired by the example of the colonies to the north, wished to prevent the act from going into operation. The usual strategy was to take steps to seize and destroy the stamps and to force the agent to resign. These radicals called themselves Sons of Liberty; Governor Wright called them "Sons of Licentiousness."[8] For ten years they were to be the bane of his existence and the particular object of his contempt. The Liberty Boys held their first open meeting at Machenry's tavern on Monday, October 28. They agreed that as soon as the stampmaster should arrive in the colony, they would go to see him and put such a scare into him that he would resign his office. No plans to destroy the stamps were made.[9]

6. *Ibid.*

7. This estimate of the temper of the colonial leaders is largely based on the testimony of honest James Habersham, whose word, in view of his support of the Stamp Act and of his position in the colony, can certainly be relied upon in this instance. See Ga. Hist. Soc., *Colls.*, VI, 44-46.

8. Wright to Henry Seymour Conway, Mar. 15, 1766, unpub. Col. Records, XXXVII, 123.

9. Wright to Conway, Jan. 31, 1766, *ibid.*, 103-9; *Ga. Gaz.*, Oct. 31, 1765.

Although neither the stamps nor the agent had in fact arrived, the Liberty people were not sure but that Wright was keeping both hidden to be produced dramatically on November 1. On the thirtieth of October five gentlemen got letters purportedly from the "inhabitants of the town of Savannah" accusing them either of being the agent for the stamp tax or of having the stamps in their possession. They were ordered to tell what they knew about the matter by advertising at the "Exchange, the Market, and the Pump." "The fatal consequences" attendant on their refusal to comply were hinted at. Three of the men promptly disclaimed any knowledge of the business. A fourth, Denys Rolle, a member of Parliament then in Savannah, immediately decided that the time had come for him to go back to England. And the fifth, James Habersham, ignored the letter. It was at this point that Governor Wright entered the fray. He issued a proclamation offering fifty pounds reward for the names of the letter writers.[10] Wishing to "shew becoming Detestation and just Abhorence of such malignant Practices," the Assembly promptly and unanimously voted to pay the reward.[11] A few days later, Governor Wright followed up this proclamation with another forbidding "all Riots, Routs and tumultuous Assemblies."[12] "From this time," Wright later wrote, "the spirit of Faction & Sedition took place & increased."[13]

Exactly what he privately thought of the Stamp Act, James Wright chose to keep to himself. Although neither when the act was being prepared nor at any later time did he offer one word of objection to it, there is a good deal to indicate that, certainly at first, he shared the general opinion that the tax was ill-advised. Clues to the Governor's attitude can be found in his treatment of the House of Assembly in the fall and winter of 1765-66. The Assembly, in session all during the troubles,

10. *Ga. Gaz.*, Oct. 31, Nov. 14, 1765.
11. Journal of Assembly, Oct. 31, 1765, *Col. Records*, XIV, 278.
12. Minutes of Gov. and Council, Nov. 12, 1765, *ibid.*, IX, 439.
13. Wright to Conway, Jan. 31, 1766, unpub. Col. Records, XXXVII, 103-9.

had generally a strong anti-Stamp Act bias. Drawing freely upon the enormous balance of prestige built up for his office and for himself personally during the years past, Governor Wright was able to maintain control of the Assembly and prevent its aligning Georgia with the other colonies in opposition to the tax. He claimed that he alone among the American governors "had Influence Enough to Prevent [the Assembly's] even attempting to make any Resolves as to the Rights and Privileges Claimed by the americans, and also any applications Relative to the Non Execution of the Stamp Act."[14]   This boast was not entirely accurate. On two occasions the Assembly did show its dislike for the Stamp Act. Wright's silence, his tacit acquiescence, strongly suggest that his energetic enforcement of the law was inspired rather by his determination to maintain order and uphold the authority of the British government than by any personal approval of the law itself.

Late in August the speaker of the House of Assembly, Alexander Wylly, got a circular letter from the Massachusetts legislature inviting the Assembly of Georgia to send delegates to a congress in New York to protest the passage of the Stamp Act and petition for its repeal. Wylly promptly asked the Governor to call the legislature into session. When Wright refused, Wylly sent expresses to all parts of the colony with messages to the members of the Assembly suggesting they come to Savannah. Sixteen turned up and on September 2 drew up a reply to the Massachusetts speaker in which they highly approved the aims of the proposed congress but regretfully informed him they could not send representatives because officially the Assembly was in recess. What Wylly had done, in effect, was to usurp the governor's sole right to convene the legislature. Wright made no official protest at the time; he took no notice of it in his letters to the Board of Trade. Given Wright's known attachment to his prerogatives and his

14. Wright to Board of Trade, Mar. 10, 1766, *ibid.*, XXVIII, Part 2, 322; Wright to Conway, Mar. 10, 1766, *ibid.*, XXXVII, 116-18.

insistence upon legal and constitutional forms, his silence in this matter amounted to complicity. When the Assembly met in October, it thanked "Mr Speaker for the extraordinary Care and Trouble he has been pleased to take on this very interesting and important Occasion," and later voted to sign the memorial and petitions adopted by the Stamp Act Congress. During all of this, the Governor said not a word.[15]

Governor Wright also came close to active cooperation with the Assembly in the replacement of his friend William Knox as colonial agent because of Knox's stand on the Stamp Act. It was strongly hinted that Wright was not at all pleased with his friend's published letter defending the tax.[16] The Assembly, showing itself to be a great deal less than pleased either with the letter or with Knox, voted in November to inform their agent "that this Province hath no further Occasion for his Service."[17] The Governor did not raise a finger in Knox's behalf. Instead he proposed to the legislature another man as a suitable successor. Failing to get the Council to abandon Knox, the Assembly set up its own committee to correspond with Charles Garth, whom it employed to act as agent for the remainder of Knox's term.[18] Wright, uncharacteristically, allowed this unusual arrangement to go unnoted and unchallenged, to his later regret.

Even more revealing were Wright's relations with the Council and, in particular, with its president, James Habersham. The Council, not enthusiastic about the act itself, vigorously supported the Governor in its enforcement. Habersham made it clear in his letters to William Knox that his opinions with regard to the Stamp Act were those of the Council. There is great reason to believe that they were also Wright's. And Habersham firmly believed that the Act was a terrible mistake.

15. Journal of Assembly, Oct. 29, Nov. 25, Dec. 2, 14, 16, 1765, *Col. Records*, XIV, 270-74, 300-1, 304-5, 315-16, 317-18.
16. Habersham to Knox, Oct. 28, 1765, Ga. Hist. Soc., *Colls.*, VI, 44-46.
17. Journal of Assembly, Nov. 15, 1765, *Col. Records*, XIV, 293.
18. Journal of Assembly, Oct. 28, 1765, ff., *ibid.*, 268, 316-19, 327, 329, 336-37, 358.

James Habersham held a unique position in the colony and in his relations with the Governor. He had come with George Whitefield from England to Georgia in its early days and had established himself as one of the first and most successful merchants in Savannah. In 1765, Habersham, by now more a planter than merchant, owned thousands of acres and scores of slaves. For many years he had been a stable and highly respected figure in the political life of the colony. An assistant and colonial secretary under the Trustees, he had in 1754 taken a seat on the Council of the new royal government. Reynolds had had no more effective opponent than Habersham, and he was probably one of Ellis's closest colonial advisers, certainly Wright's. Essentially a simple man, Habersham had the wisdom that sometimes comes after long experience to men of strong character and genuine good will. To him, the Stamp Act was wrong in principle and unwise as policy. But any thought of defying the act was immeasurably worse. He believed, mistakenly in part, that the disorders in America would only bolster the determination of Parliament to impose an American tax, making repeal impossible. What really led Habersham to risk his personal safety to support the enforcement of the tax was his conviction that it was his duty as a British subject, made ten times more binding by his being a royal officer, to give his obedience to his government.[19]

Habersham and Wright had both lost their wives and the two widowers, intimate friends, spent many hours together each day. When the going was at its roughest in late January 1766, Habersham went so far as to make plans for moving into the governor's house with Wright.[20] There can be no question of their complete agreement as to the course of action to be pursued in enforcing the Stamp Act. Each went out of his way to signify approval of the other's conduct. In June 1766, Governor Wright officially reported that Habersham had

19. Ga. Hist. Soc., *Colls.*, VI, 44-50, 53-58.
20. *Ibid.*, 26-27, 39, 56.

"behaved extremely well towards the support of Government
& Authority" and had "taken great pains to assist" him "on the
late Occasion."[21]   Habersham, even freer in his praise, wrote
George Whitefield: "Our honest Governor has on this Critical
occasion behaved like himself, I mean like a man of honor and
a faithful Servant of the Crown."[22]   It is inconceivable that the
two men should have had any markedly different opinions
about the utility or the wisdom of the Act.   But for both,
personal opinions were at this juncture beside the point.   As
Habersham expressed it, "The Crown have as good a right to
faithfull servants, as you and I have to those we pay wages to."[23]

   Whatever his private feelings, Governor Wright sought and
got the aid of the Council in enforcing the Act and forestalled
any overt move against it in the House of Assembly; but the
main drama of the Stamp Act in Georgia was acted out not in
the chambers of the legislature but on the streets of Savannah.
Here the Governor was less successful in keeping quiet what
was variously known and hazily identified as the Sons of
Liberty, the Liberty Boys, the Mob, or the Inhabitants of
Savannah.   These, too, Wright triumphed over, but only after
many anxious days and at a dear price.   On November 1, 1765,
the day set for the sale of the stamped paper, the Governor
was in a quandary.   There was no stamped paper in Savannah,
no agent, and Wright did not even have official notice of the
passage of the Act.   On the advice of the Council he closed the
land office and suspended the courts.   The port of Savannah he
kept open by the expedient of granting passes for vessels to
leave the harbor.   Since ships now began to be diverted to
Savannah from the closed ports of the other colonies, the river
was soon crowded with vessels from all over the Empire.[24]

   21. Wright to Conway, June 24, 1766, unpub. Col. Records, XXXVII, 97-98.
   22. Jan. 27, 1766, Ga. Hist. Soc., *Colls.*, VI, 55.
   23. *Ibid.*
   24. Minutes of Gov. and Council, Oct. 31, Nov. 22, 1765, *Col. Records*, IX,
435, 439-40; Wright to Board of Trade, Nov. 9, 1765, unpub. Col. Records,
XXVIII, Part 2, 292-93; Habersham to Knox, Dec. 4, 1765, Ga. Hist. Soc.,
Colls., VI, 49-50; Habersham to Daniel Roubadeau, Dec. [Jan.] 17, 1766, *ibid.*,
57-58.

During the month of November, Governor Wright kept busy preparing to enforce the sale of the stamped paper whenever it and an agent should arrive. He knew that the Liberty Boys were holding secret meetings and laying plans to thwart him by seizing the stamps and intimidating the agent.[25] Consequently, he and the Council made arrangements to store the stamps in the guardhouse and to give the stampmaster what protection they could.[26] Of the 120 Rangers stationed at five posts about the colony, Wright called into Savannah fifty-six men and eight officers. In speeches and private conversations he worked hard to persuade the colonists of the rashness of violent and unlawful opposition to the laws of Parliament.[27] His main task, as he saw it, was to counteract the "Inflamatory Papers letters & messages continually sent to the People" in Georgia "from the Liberty Boys . . . in Charles Town," who were contemptuous of the timidity of the Georgians and infuriated by the sight of Savannah's taking over the shipping normally belonging to Charleston.[28]

When Governor Wright finally got a copy of the act "in a Private way," he posted abstracts of it in appropriate offices, and on November 22 took the requisite oath.[29] A week later the collectors of the customs got official copies of the act, and by December 4 the port of Savannah was closed.[30] Not until December 5 did the *Speedwell* come up the river with the stamped paper aboard. When news of this got about Savannah that afternoon, the "Inhabitants of the Town" met and authorized several gentlemen to go to Governor Wright and inform him

25. Wright to Board of Trade, Dec. 2, 1765, unpub. Col. Records, XXVIII, Part 2, 287-98; Wright to Conway, Jan. 31, 1766, *ibid.*, XXXVII, 103-9.
26. Minutes of Gov. and Council, Nov. 12, 1765, *Col. Records*, IX, 438-39.
27. Wright to Board of Trade, Jan. 15, 1766, unpub. Col. Records, XXVIII, Part 2, 303-7.
28. Wright to Conway, Jan. 31, 1766, *ibid.*, XXXVII, 103-9; *S. C. Gaz.; And Country Jour.*, Feb. 25, 1766.
29. Wright to Board of Trade, Dec. 2, 1765, unpub. Col. Records, XXVIII, Part 2, 297-98; Minutes of Gov. and Council, Nov. 22, 1765, *Col. Records*, IX, 439.
30. Minutes of Gov. and Council, Dec. 16, 1765, *Col. Records*, IX, 455; Habersham to Knox, Dec. 4, 1765, Ga. Hist. Soc., *Colls.*, VI, 49-50.

that they "at that time" had no intention of taking or destroying the stamps.   On this assurance Wright and the Council decided to alter their plan to store the papers in the guardhouse and instead to deposit them with the commissary at the warehouse used to store the Indian presents.   The controversial paper was brought ashore the next day without incident.[31]

In December, at least sixty seagoing ships were anchored up and down the river opposite Savannah, tied up by Wright's order closing the port.   Some were ready to put to sea; some were only partly loaded.[32]   This being the time of year for new rice to begin to come into town, the merchants and masters of the ships, frantic at the prospect of the cargoes spoiling on idle ships manned by idle crews, petitioned Wright to allow the ships to sail.   The Council unanimously advised the governor on December 16 that he could not legally clear the vessels without using the stamped paper.   This barrier became insurmountable when the Council voted five to four against advising Wright to appoint a temporary agent to act for the regular one, a Mr. Angus, until he should arrive from Britain. Two days later, however, the Council reversed itself by approving the appointment of an agent *pro tem* provided there should be a "general application" for one.[33]   Accepting this implied invitation, the merchants of the town put into circulation a petition for that purpose.[34]   Practical considerations had made them abandon their initial opposition to the collection of the stamp tax.   Such was the state of affairs at the turn of the year.

Now that the merchants of Savannah were actually asking that the stamp tax be collected, the Liberty people could no longer afford to remain quiet.   To wait until the regular agent had arrived before striking might prove fatal to their cause.

31. Minutes of Gov. and Council, Dec. 6, 1765, *Col. Records*, IX, 453-54; Wright to Conway, Jan. 31, 1766, unpub. Col. Records, XXXVII, 103-9.
32. Habersham to Roubadeau, Dec. [Jan.] 17, 1766, Ga. Hist. Soc., *Colls.*, VI, 58.
33. Minutes of Gov. and Council, *Col. Records*, IX, 454-60.
34. *Pa. Gaz.*, Feb. 13, 1766.

At about three o'clock on Thursday afternoon, January 2, Captain Milledge and Captain Powell of the Rangers came up to Governor Wright with the news that nearly two hundred Liberty Boys had already assembled in the town and more were gathering fast.[35] The report was that they were planning to break open the store and take the stamped papers. Wright ordered the officers to assemble their men and meet him at the guardhouse. Taking down his musket, the Governor went over to take charge of the troops. From the guardhouse, he saw a large group of men with colors and drums milling around the gate of his home. Walking toward the house with musket still in hand, Wright pushed ahead until he stood in the middle of the crowd. Then he demanded to know what they were up to. Some of the men called out asking if he intended to appoint a stamp distributor as the merchants' petition requested.

Wright answered at some length. Pointing out that this was hardly "the manner to wait upon the governor of a province," he told them that he had as yet got no such request but that in any case they could be assured that he would keep his oath to His Majesty as he understood it.[36] Then he made a point that was a favorite with him—although they called themselves Sons of Liberty, the time would soon come when they would realize that he was the real defender of liberty and that their actions were destructive to it. After hearing Wright out, the Liberty Boys began to disperse with the intention of reassembling at a moment's notice should a stampmaster be appointed.

Governor Wright, returning to the guardhouse, mustered

35. The following account of the disturbance of January 2 and the arrival of the stampmaster is pieced together from two letters written by Wright describing the incident and from a more detailed letter written by one of the Liberty Boys on January 6. There is no contradiction at any point between the accounts of the two opponents, but each includes details omitted by the other. *Pa. Gaz.*, Feb. 13, 1766; Wright to Board of Trade, Jan. 15, 1766, unpub. Col. Records, XXVIII, Part 2, 303-7; Wright to Conway, Jan. 31, 1766, *ibid.*, XXXVII, 103-9.

36. *Pa. Gaz.*, Feb. 13, 1766.

fifty-four Rangers and marched with them to the store at Fort Halifax on the outskirts of town.   There he had the stamped papers loaded on a cart and hauled back to the guard-house.   The Rangers were left to stand watch over the papers while the Governor with a crew of forty-odd men patrolled the streets.   It was nearly five o'clock in the afternoon before Wright had got the papers safely stored, and not until nine that night did he think it safe for him to go inside.

As soon as the Governor had gone home, the patrol, com-posed of merchants, their clerks, and several shipmasters, drifted into a tavern.   Everything was pleasant enough until a tipsy Liberty Boy stumbled in.   Not satisfied with booting him out, some of the clerks set about to give him a sound thrashing in the dark outside.   Excited by the wine and their sport, the clerks forced their way into another room of the tavern where a party of Liberty Boys, like the merchants, was engaged "in the wars of Bacchus."[37]   Swinging their guns, the clerks fell to cracking heads—all of which did nothing to lessen the resent-ment against either the merchants or the Stamp Act.

After spending the night fully clothed, Governor Wright got news at lunch time the next day that the stamp distributor was at Tybee waiting to come up to town.   Mr. Angus could hardly have picked a worse time to put in an appearance.   It was Monday night of the next week before the good Governor again put on his nightshirt.   Wright, who had long since made certain that he would be the first in Savannah to hear of the agent's arrival at Tybee, immediately sent the scout boat down the river, manned by an officer and party of Rangers.   The officer's instructions were to allow no one to speak to Mr. Angus until he was safely in the Governor's house.   At noon on Saturday, January 4, the boat put the stampmaster ashore a little below the town.   Several gentlemen, who were waiting for him there, conducted him as unobtrusively as possible to Wright's home.

37. *Ibid*

After being outfaced by the Governor on the second, the Liberty Boys in Savannah had become discouraged. The swift and efficient way that Wright had whisked the stamped papers and then the distributor out of their reach impressed them. Overawed by the Governor and his Rangers, they despaired of halting the operation of the tax. On Tuesday, January 7, Governor Wright reopened the ports of Savannah and Sunbury in conformity with the Stamp Act. The merchants and the disheartened leaders of the Liberty people at Savannah had come to some sort of agreement: the merchants signed a pledge not to apply for any papers not necessary for shipping; in return, the Liberty Boys agreed to offer no objections to the use of stamped paper by the customs officials.[38]

While Savannah was settling down to a state of uneasy peace, news of the arrival of the stamp distributor and of the reopening of the ports was just penetrating the back-country. Later in the week disquieting rumors began to drift into Savannah. The word was that the friends of Liberty in the country were taking up their arms and coming together at different places all over the province. Governor Wright at once sent expresses with letters to "Many of the most Sensible & dispassionate People" outside Savannah, exhorting them to step forward and persuade their neighbors to return to their homes. The Governor expressed gratification that his "weight & Credit was Sufficient to Check & Prevent all Commotions & disturbances in the Country," and by the middle of January everything seemed quiet and easy.[39]

All of Wright's high hopes of having brought the Liberty Boys to terms, if not to their senses, were blasted during the last few days of January when he again got reports of a really serious nature from the country. "Some Incendiaries from

38. Ga. Hist. Soc., *Colls.*, VI, 55, 58; Wright to Thomas Gage, Jan. 20, 1766, Thomas Gage Papers, William L. Clements Library. All Gage Papers cited herein are from the American Series.

39. Wright to Board of Trade, Jan. 15, 1766, unpub. Col. Records, XXVIII, Part 2, 303-7.

Charles Town" "full fraught with Sedition & Rebellion," as Wright put it, had been at work in the backcountry of Georgia. So successful had they been in inflaming the country people against the Governor and the sale of stamped papers in Savannah that reportedly between six and seven hundred had armed themselves and begun to march on Savannah.[40]   By January 29, the town was in a state of "utmost confusion."   James Habersham, who had already been waylaid in the night and threatened with having his town house torn down, was secretly warned by a friend on the twenty-seventh that it would be best for him not to be found in his home two or three days thence. He accordingly made plans to leave his house in the care of his partner, and to seek refuge at the Governor's.[41]   Governor Wright now for the first time had to cope with armed men. This was the showdown.   With the decision of who should call the tune in Georgia—the Governor or the Liberty Boys—hinging on his actions for the next few days, Governor Wright did a bold thing.   He very nearly stripped the town of its defenses.   The stamped paper had become a symbol so far beyond its practical importance that Wright sent it down with fifty of his Rangers and two subalterns to Fort George on Cockspur Island where it would be safe.[42]   Then, while their "very Flesh" trembled, the Governor's supporters in Savannah awaited the expected visit from the Liberty Boys on the thirty-first.[43]

The day passed without any sign of the men camped seven miles from the town.   Governor Wright believed that "with the assistance of Some well disposed Gent[n]" he had induced a large number to turn back, but he estimated that there were still more than three hundred armed men just over the horizon

---

40. Wright to Conway, Jan. 31, 1766, *ibid.*, XXXVII, 103-9; Wright to Board of Trade, Feb. 1, 1766, *ibid.*, XXVIII, Part 2, 314-15.

41. Habersham to George Whitefield, Jan. 27, 1766, Ga. Hist. Soc., *Colls.*, VI, 54-55; Habersham to Knox, Jan. 29, 1766, *ibid.*, 56.

42. Wright to Conway, Jan. 31, 1766, unpub. Col. Records, XXXVII, 103-9; Wright to Gage, Feb. 1, 1766, Gage Papers, Clements Lib.

43. Habersham to Whitefield, Jan. 27, 1766, Ga. Hist. Soc., *Colls.*, VI, 54.

from the town gates.[44]   The show of force was intended to extort from the Governor a promise that no more stamped paper would be issued until an answer to the colonists' petitions to the King had been received.   The plan was for the armed men to surround the Governor's home and, some reportedly said, shoot him if he proved stubborn.   The townspeople feared that the mob would also take their revenge on the persons and property of those who had supported the Governor.   February 1 was a day of tense uncertainty for Governor Wright.[45]   But on the second he got welcome news that changed the entire picture.   Captain Fanshawe of the *Speedwell* had kept his promise to return and was at the moment in the river with his ship.   Wright quickly had the stamped paper transferred from the fort to the man-of-war.   The fifty Rangers then lost no time in coming back up to town.   The Governor was now ready for the Liberty Boys.

It was the fourth of February before the Liberty Boys finally marched in and mustered with arms and colors on the town common.   They had come too late.   With twenty sailors from the *Speedwell* to reinforce his Rangers, Governor Wright had nearly one hundred trained men at his ready disposal.   Faced with this force, the Liberty Boys began disputing among themselves.   Three hours later they were gone.   To save face they boasted in parting that their friends in South Carolina had promised to send over four or five hundred men and that they would return with their augmented force.[46]

At this point Wright was confident that by talking to "some of the most dispassionate People & of the most considerable

44. Wright to Board of Trade, Feb. 1, 1766, unpub. Col. Records, XXVIII, Part 2, 314-15; Wright to Conway, Mar. 10, 1766, *ibid.*, XXXVII, 116-18; Wright to Gage, Feb. 1, 1766, Gage Papers, Clements Lib.

45. Habersham to Whitefield, Jan. 27, 1766, Ga. Hist. Soc., *Colls.*, VI, 54-55; Wright to Board of Trade, Feb. 1, 7, 1766, unpub. Col. Records, XXVIII, Part 2, 314-15, 317-18; Wright to Conway, Feb. 7, 1766, *ibid.*, XXXVII, 110-11; Wright to Gage, Feb. 1, 1766, Gage Papers, Clements Lib.

46. Wright to Board of Trade, Feb. 7, 1766, unpub. Col. Records, XXVIII, Part 2, 317-18; Wright to Conway, Feb. 7, 1766, *ibid.*, XXXVII, 110-11.

property" among the Liberty folk he could bring the colony to its senses and persuade most of the Liberty Boys to submit to his authority, provided that the threat of reinforcements from South Carolina did not materialize.[47]   The whole affair had reached nightmare proportions for him in January.   The lawlessness, disorder, insolence, and insults that he experienced left their mark on Governor Wright.   He could find little consolation in the fact that he was winning out over the Sons of Liberty.   That a wretched mob had dared, and so nearly with success, to attempt to wrest from his hands the authority vested in him by the King was, for Wright, "a Matter my Lord too Cutting for a good Subject & Servant to Bear."[48]

The ignominious withdrawal of the Liberty Boys from the town common on February 4 marked the end of the threat of mob rule in Savannah.   One other affair a week or so later was managed so furtively that Governor Wright knew nothing of it for several days afterwards.   While the Liberty Boys were still camped before the town, Wright had received a letter from Henry Seymour Conway, the secretary of state for the Southern Department.   The letter, the first since the trouble started, was conciliatory but it warned the colonists that their views would not be advanced by mob violence.   Always punctiliously correct, the Governor went before the Council to read Conway's letter while the mob was, almost literally, howling at the gates. Apparently the letter carried weight, for Wright wrote home that the Liberty Boys in South Carolina went to great lengths to brand it a forgery.   At any rate, several nights later "some of the very Lower Class," lacking that sense of timing which told their leaders that the moment for violence had passed, burnt in effigy Conway and his letter.   After having himself been so long badgered by the people, Governor Wright, though shocked, betrayed a certain satisfaction in informing Secretary Conway in faraway London that his dummy figure had been

47. Wright to Conway, Feb. 7, 1766, *ibid.*, XXXVII, 110-11.
48. Wright to Board of Trade, Jan. 15, 1766, *ibid.*, XXVIII, Part 2, 303-7.

burned atop a pile of brush on the sandy streets of Savannah.[49]

The Liberty Boys had hardly dispersed on February 4 when the vagaries of South Carolina once again moved Wright to rage. This time it was not the Liberty Boys of Charleston but the Governor of South Carolina who seemingly threatened to upset once again the precarious equilibrium in Georgia. Lieutenant Governor Bull decided to reopen the port of Charleston on the grounds that no stamped paper was available. Sedition from the people was bad enough, Wright felt, but to be stabbed in the back by a fellow governor was too much. Wright flatly stated, though mistakenly, that Bull had the stamped papers under lock and key in Charleston. All of the tumult and strife in Georgia he had always maintained could be traced back to one place—Charleston. The excesses of the Liberty Boys in South Carolina, he charged, had gone unchecked since October without the least sign even of disapproval from Governor Bull. Although he feared that Bull's last act of leniency contrasted with his own firmness would "raise the People in arms again," Wright heard only murmurings from his province.[50]

Soon he began to see signs that his campaign to win over the Liberty people was gaining headway. He was making an intensive effort to follow up with persuasion the victory which superior force had given him on February 4. Calling in those leaders of the Liberty movement whom he thought most sensible, Wright talked to them long and earnestly of the dangers and likely consequences of their arming a mob in opposition to regular authority. Once confident that he had convinced them, he sent these men back into the country with instructions to meet with their neighbors and explain to them what the Governor had said. Early in March, letters began to come in from

49. Wright to Conway, Mar. 15, Jan. 31, 1766, *ibid.*, XXXVII, 123, 103-9; Minutes of Gov. and Council, Feb. 3, 1766, *Col. Records*, IX, 470; Wright to Gage, Mar. 15, 1766, Gage Papers, Clements Lib.

50. Wright to Board of Trade, Feb. 10, Mar. 10, 1766, unpub. Col. Records, XXVIII, Part 2, 320, 322; Wright to Conway, Mar. 10, 1766, *ibid.*, XXXVII, 116-18.

all over the province indicating that a strong wave of reaction against the violence of the past two months had set in. The leaders of the Liberty people in the country assured him, Wright said, that "let the consequences of the Stamp Act, be what it may, they never will appear in arms again, or oppose His Majesties authority."[51]

Three months later, Governor Wright had one final galling experience. He saw his hard-won victory over the Liberty Boys brought to nothing by news of repeal of the Stamp Act. Taking heart from what seemed a vindication of their methods and ignoring the Declaratory Act by which Parliament reasserted its sovereignty in America, the unrepentant among the Liberty Boys seized upon the tidings to spread the report that Wright's overzealous enforcement of the Stamp Act had met with disapproval at home. Rumors of his imminent removal circulated about the province.[52] Although assured by Shelburne that these reports were false, Governor Wright got no praise from him for his loyalty and effectiveness in enforcing the Stamp Act. Instead there was the gentle reminder that a governor must always act in such a way as not to give the impression of restraining the "just & decent Exercise of that Liberty which belongs to the People."[53] With understandable heat, Wright intimated to Shelburne that he needed no such advice and suggested that Shelburne might possibly find *"Just & Decent liberty"* in England was one thing and in America another.[54]

The humiliations and triumphs of the year 1766 did something to James Wright. Perhaps it would be too dramatic to say that this critical year put iron in his soul; but no one would deny that he came out of the Stamp Act troubles a stronger and more distinct personality. The passage of the Stamp Act, the colonial opposition to it, and its repeal combined to leave

51. Wright to Conway, Mar. 10, 1766, *ibid.,* XXXVII, 116-18.
52. Wright to Conway, June 24, 1766, *ibid.,* 97-98; Minutes of Gov. and Council, June 16, 1766, *Col. Records,* IX, 540.
53. Shelburne to Wright, Sept. 22, 1766, unpub. Col. Records, XXXVII, 126-27.
54. Wright to Shelburne, Jan. 3, 1767, *ibid.,* 174-75.

Wright disillusioned—disillusioned both as to the wisdom and power of the British government and as to the loyalty and good sense of the people. There is not a scrap of evidence that Wright at any time before 1765 overtly questioned any decision of the Board of Trade; after 1765 he disagreed with these gentlemen often enough. Until 1765 the colonial leaders had been his trusted partners in the affairs of government; from 1766 until the Revolution they were either his allies or they were his adversaries, to be watched, outwitted, and overcome.

But whatever confidence he lost in others he gained in himself. Every other governor on the continent had had to make concessions to the Liberty Boys of his colony. "You," wrote General Gage, "are the only Gover[n] from the Province of Massachusetts Bay to Georgia, who has Enforced the Law in one Instance,"[55] "the only Governor from Boston to Savannah who has not been obliged to yield to the Torrent of Popular Fury."[56] Parliament itself had been forced to beat a hasty retreat. Amid so much weakness and bumbling, Governor Wright saw himself as a shining exception. Had he not successfully withstood every onslaught of the Liberty people, not yielding "an Inch to the phrenzy of an unthinking Mutitude [*sic*]"?[57] His letters to the Board of Trade, crisper and more to the point, are the letters of a new man. His loyalty and devotion to duty were unimpaired, even strengthened, but they were no longer blind. In the turbulent days shortly before the Revolution, no false modesty kept Sir James from inquiring of the Board if he were not needed in London to advise his Majesty's ministers on American affairs. And his increased confidence manifested itself in his relations with the colonists by a certain omniscient air which sometimes became impatient, haughty, and uncompromising.

55. Gage to Wright, Apr. 26, 1766, Gage Papers, Clements Lib.
56. Gage to Wright, Apr. [?] 30, 1766, *ibid.*
57. Ga. Hist. Soc., *Colls.*, VI, 56; Wright to Gage, Jan. 20, 1766, Gage Papers, Clements Lib.

Although his Stamp Act victories made him personally a stronger man, a man with a greater amount of tangible power at his command, Wright's general position had been weakened. In a sense he had liquidated many of his hoarded assets in subduing the Liberty Boys. The coin of good will, trust, and gratitude could be spent but once. James Wright emerged as the powerful leader of a powerful faction, but gone forever was his position as leader of a united colony once unanimity of opinion had been destroyed.

Governor Wright was well aware that the Stamp Act had altered the political situation in the colony, perhaps permanently. He was never under the least misapprehension that the spirit raised by the Stamp Act was ended either by his suppression of the Liberty party or by the repeal of the Act itself. Early in February he expressed doubt to Conway that he would be able to place "intire confidence in the People for some time."[58] One week after he had announced the repeal of the Stamp Act Wright wrote more fully of this:

. . . after the People in a Country have been inflamed to the highest degree . . . from almost one End of the Continent to the other . . . its not to be supposed or expected that all Heats & Party Spirit can subside at once. time & prudent Conduct can only effect that, and this Province is not without some violent Republican Spirits, full of rancour against the Government & Parliament, and still fix't in their strange mistaken Ideas of Liberty, and that no Power can tax or restrain them &c but themselves or Representatives of their own choosing. . . .[59]

Writing in the same vein in July he confided his fear that these "Republican Spirits" would "rather cherish those Ideas, than recede from them."[60]

The Stamp Act disturbances opened no chasm in Georgia politics, left no irreconcilable forces arrayed one against the other. But the passage of the hated Stamp Act by Parliament,

58. Wright to Conway, Feb. 7, 1766, unpub. Col. Records, XXXVII, 110-11.
59. Wright to Conway, June 24, 1766, *ibid.*, 97-98.
60. Wright to Conway, July 23, 1766, *ibid.*, 129-30; Wright to Gage, July 10, Nov. 18, 1766, Gage Papers, Clements Lib.

its enforcement by Governor Wright, and its defiance by the colonists inevitably focused attention on the whole structure of the Empire. For a moment, people found themselves perforce taking a deliberate, if not disinterested, look at the political system under which they lived. Matter-of-fact acceptance and wholehearted admiration gave way to vague questioning, doubt, suspicion, dissatisfaction, and in some instances, to outright hostility. The Stamp Act made it clear to many Georgians that the underlying justification for the imperial system—that what was good for the Empire was of necessity good for Georgia—was not always so. Presumably Parliament was persuaded that the tax was good for the Empire. There was nobody in the colony who thought it good for Georgia. Once doubt had been cast on the truth of the axiom, it became difficult to accept it again on faith.

Whatever else it did, the Stamp Act in Georgia fathered something very like a party of opposition in the House of Assembly, a faction which stood ready to oppose unpopular policies of the royal government and to compete with it for power. This faction, vague in outline and unorganized, at times aggressively pushing its claims, and again quiescent—almost non-existent—remained to remind Governor Wright when need be that there were limits beyond which he could not go unchallenged. It took for itself the role of defender of the rights and liberties of the people. The House faction supporting the government, with Governor Wright its leader and proud symbol, stood for the preservation of law and order, for the protection of person and property, to Wright's mind the only guarantees of true liberty. One supposedly abridged the rights of the people; the other subverted law and order. The line was drawn. Intermittently for the next ten years the pressure of events tended to drive men to one side or the other. Hereafter the leaders of Georgia found it more and more difficult simply to pursue their personal political ambitions and to confine their differences to squabbles over local issues and personal rivalries. The stresses and strains of an empire were casting them in the roles of protagonists for one or another of two great divergent and hostile points of view. Principle had raised its ugly head in Georgia politics. When the day arrived that a man had no alternative but to choose between freedom and oppression, law and anarchy, when every man had to declare himself either Patriot or Loyalist, Rebel or Tory, civil war and revolution were at hand.

But such a pass was still a decade away. The Stamp Act probably took Georgia less far down the road to revolution than it did the other colonies, but Georgia had farther to go. The deeper significance of the winter of 1765-66 for Georgia lies in its effect upon the character of James Wright, the dominant figure in Georgia for another decade, and in the subtle but very real reorientation of colonial politics which pointed Georgia in a new direction, even if it failed to move it far.

CHAPTER VI

Governor Wright and the House of Assembly: The Challenge, 1766-1768

GOVERNOR WRIGHT, who had not been enthusiastic about the imposition of a stamp tax in the fall of 1765, was even less happy about its repeal in the spring of 1766. This show of weakness in the face of mob violence filled Wright with gloomy forebodings. When he called the House of Assembly into session in November 1766, he was not at all certain what the consequences would be, despite the fact that most of the assemblymen had been elected in the happy year 1764 and had for two years worked well with him, even to remaining surprisingly docile during the Stamp Act tumults. He was immediately reassured, however, when the House quietly settled down to routine business and all was calm until the Christmas recess.[1]

About the middle of January, shortly after the assemblymen had returned from their holiday, Governor Wright got a letter from Captain Ralph Phillips, commander of the King's detachment of troops in Georgia, asking for the provisions due his troops under the Quartering Act. The Quartering Act, passed in 1765 and designed to make the colonists contribute to the garrisoning and supplying of British troops stationed in America, had assumed after the repeal of the Stamp Act the

1. Wright to [Shelburne], Jan. 5, Apr. 6, 1767, unpub. Col. Records, XXXVII, 154-56, 177-90.

proportions of a major grievance in America, particularly in New York. Wright's tactfully worded request that the legislature comply with the Act met with a friendly reception in the upper house but evoked no response from the Assembly. The House of Assembly referred the Governor's message to a committee and there it remained.[2] This move, Wright was certain, was taken to allow the House time to get advice from South Carolina. At the end of about three weeks, he prodded the Assembly by hinting to two of its members that unless the Assembly acted soon it might well hear words from him that "would not be pleasing" to it.[3] His suspicion that nothing was going to be done about supplying the required provisions was confirmed a day or two later, on February 18, when the Assembly informed the Governor that it would be unable to grant his request because to do so would be a betrayal of trust to its constituency and would set a dangerous precedent as well.[4] Mindful of Shelburne's implied rebuke for his zealous enforcement of the Stamp Act, Governor Wright contented himself with replying that he would make a report of the Assembly's actions to the King's ministers.

The refusal of the House of Assembly to implement the Quartering Act suggested early in 1767 what the future held in store for Governor Wright. This piece of defiance on the part of the Assembly represented more than a passing disagreement between the Governor and the lower house of the legislature on this particular issue. It heralded the initial appearance of a persisting political faction independent of the Governor, a faction of the Assembly out to challenge Wright's leadership and to advance its claims, willy-nilly, at his expense.

Tension and conflict between the Assembly and the royal governor was nothing new or unusual; it was in the very nature

2. Journal of Assembly, Jan. 20, 28, 1767, *Col. Records*, XIV, 412-14, 420; Journal of Upper House, Jan. 20, 1767, *ibid.*, XVII, 312.
3. Wright to Shelburne, Apr. 6, 1767, unpub. Col. Records, XXXVII, 177-90; Wright to Gage, Feb. 25, 1767, Gage Papers, Clements Lib.
4. *Col. Records*, XIV, 441.

of things. In Britain's royal colonies in America, the conventional rivalry between legislature and executive was inevitably intensified by the fact that the popularly elected assemblies were always free to take the provincial point of view on every issue while the governor was bound sometimes to set the claims of his king against the claims of his province. Both Ellis and Wright recognized and took into account this threat of friction. Even in the halcyon days of political peace which Ellis inaugurated and which Wright enjoyed until after 1765, the governor took care to use his political arts and his power to keep the lower house of the legislature in line. Both Ellis and Wright cooperated with the House of Assembly and sought its cooperation, but neither was ever so foolish as to rely upon cooperation being freely given or freely received by the lower house. Each clasped the appointed Council to his bosom, and between the two they dominated the colonial legislature. In a sense, the remarkable thing is not that a party of opposition appeared in 1767 but that its appearance was so long delayed.

From its inception the Liberty party dominated the House of Assembly, and after 1768 its dominance there went virtually unchallenged, even by Wright. Secure in their control of the lower house, the Liberty people stubbornly sought to enlarge the power of the House at the expense of Governor Wright and of his vulnerable ally, the Council. In all this, they seemingly followed the pattern set in the other colonies as America moved toward revolution. Yet the Liberty party in Georgia was both more and less than simply the evolving party of revolution. Governor Wright's struggle with the Georgia Assembly between 1767 and 1774 looks on the surface like a reflection in miniature of what was going on at the same time in Massachusetts where Governor Francis Barnard and later Thomas Hutchinson were fighting to stem the rising tide of revolution in the Massachusetts General Court; but it would probably be more accurate, and certainly more revealing, to regard the struggle for power in Georgia more nearly in terms of what

happened in Virginia after 1688, in the days of Edmund An-
dros, Francis Nicholson, or Alexander Spotswood, all royal
governors troubled by insurgent assemblies. Governor Wright
was as much a Governor Nicholson as a Governor Hutchinson,
and the Georgia Commons House of Assembly was more the
Virginia House of Burgesses of 1700 than it was the Massachusetts General Court of 1770. The Virginia burgesses of
1688-1720 and the Georgia assemblymen of 1767-1774 were
alike seeking to clip the wings of powerful royal governors
and to extend the power of the local elected assembly at the
expense of the entrenched governor and council.

Vexing as it was, the basic political problem which plagued
Governor Wright between 1767 and 1774, though superficially
identical with the problems of the other royal governors, was
thus actually in some ways a great deal simpler, or at least more
familiar. The House of Assembly's challenge to the governor
arose in part, of course, from the same revolutionary pressures
which were undermining royal government throughout America, but more than in any other colony the assembly in
Georgia was simply responding to the much older evolutionary
pressures built up by advancing colonial wealth, self-assurance,
and political maturity. Wright was facing a problem which the
other governors had long faced, for Georgia had only now
reached a stage of development reached by the other colonies
decades before, or in some cases a century and more before.
Georgia, a mere lass among matrons, was out of phase. The
grievances and pressures which were driving the other colonies
to revolution did not operate upon Georgia with the same
urgency and immediacy, or even in the same way, that they did
elsewhere. What revolutionary spirit there was, coming as it
did largely from the outside, was fanned by the storm of excitement as much as by the winds of discontent. The young colony
of Georgia still relied heavily upon its connection with Britain
to keep safe its exposed frontiers. The mercantile regulations
of the Empire and the commercial relationships that had de-

veloped within it, far from hampering Georgia, were fostering a boom in the colony. No matter how much the Liberty gentleman of Georgia might share the revolutionary views of his fellow colonists up the coast, he was for the most part loath to jeopardize so advantageous an arrangement to support distant Massachusetts or even to win the plaudits of neighboring South Carolina.

This is not to say, of course, that the simultaneous appearance of the Liberty party in Georgia and the opposition in America to British policy was only coincidental. On the contrary, the Liberty party appeared when the rift in the British Empire, revealed by America's resistance to the Stamp Act, created a faction in the House which Governor Wright could not appease and at the same time do his duty to the King. Not only did the Stamp Act give the Liberty party birth, but the rising frenzy of opposition in America to subsequent acts of Parliament served to strengthen its hold on the Assembly, accelerate its growth, intensify its activity, give it direction, and lend it meaning far beyond its time and place. The more active leaders of the Liberty party were radicals who sought to extend the powers of the Assembly so that their policy of resistance could prevail over Wright's policy of obedience. But the point is not that they failed to make headway against Governor Wright, although they did fail, but that they were unable to impose their policy even upon the House of Assembly, almost all of whose members were nominally Liberty men. The majority of the Assembly was quite ready to grasp at the powers of the Governor or Council, but until the last they were leery of giving offense to King or Parliament. Any direct sign of disapproval from Britain was ordinarily enough to make the Assembly retrace whatever tentative steps it might have taken to range Georgia alongside her sister colonies in their fight with the mother country.

All of this goes far to explain Wright's extraordinary success in suppressing for so long revolutionary manifestations in

Georgia. Ability he had, but it was not ability alone that allowed him to emerge as relatively the strongest British governor on the continent. In so far as he had only to deal with an aggressive assembly, Wright had notable success; but when the time came for him to contend with revolution, he failed like all the rest.

That the Liberty party after 1766 was an important element in the story of Georgia there can be no doubt, but to speak today with any certainty about the functioning of this party, particularly off the floor of the House, would be difficult if not impossible. What knowledge we have of it before 1774 is derived almost entirely from the outside: from the House journals, from Wright's letters, and from occasional items in the *Georgia Gazette*. As for the individual Son of Liberty, he bobs up in the official records with increasing frequency after 1765, but not until the summer of 1774 do the records often explicitly assign him a specific identity and reveal him to be Dr. Noble Wimberly Jones, Planter Archibald Bulloch, or maybe Merchant Joseph Clay.

The journals for the session in which the Liberty faction first challenged the dominance of Governor Wright reveal that William Ewen, later to become first president of the provincial council of safety, was probably the leader of the insurgents. Ewen was strongly supported by Noble Wimberly Jones, Joseph Gibbons, John Smith, and Robert Baillie, among others. Some of these men remained in the Assembly until the last and, in the case of Jones and Smith, both of whom were at the forefront of the Liberty Boys' bid for power in the summer of 1775, there can be little doubt that they were consistent supporters of the Liberty party. But there remains the distinct possibility—and evidence for this is not entirely lacking—that more than one assemblyman was a Liberty Boy one day, a government man the next, and finally once again a Liberty Boy. For instance, Edward Telfair— Liberty Boy, Savannah merchant, important planter, and political leader during and after the Revolution—

veered from one side to another before firmly lining up with the revolutionists; Alexander Wylly and Robert Baillie, both certainly associated with the Liberty faction in the 1760's, are found to be among the loyalists once the die is cast. For the most part, the paucity of evidence tends to impose upon the group who began to challenge Governor Wright in 1767 a nameless and faceless quality which is not dispelled until the challenge takes on revolutionary implications in 1774. Then the Liberty leaders come out into the open, move toward the center of the stage, and assume for us the flesh and blood of individuality, each with his own identifiable motives, aims, and circumstances.

But the relative anonymity of the early Liberty Boy, regrettable though it is, does not pose as serious a threat to the validity of a reconstruction as it otherwise might. So completely did James Wright color developments before 1774 that the colony's tale can be told largely in terms of Wright without fatal distortion. Furthermore, for Wright (as was the case in fact) the "Liberty People" represented more than simply an ever-shifting aggregate of discontented and frustrated colonial merchants and planters in and about Savannah. The Liberty Boy was the symbol of a spirit of disrespect and change abroad in the land—a spirit that threatened the royal governor's position and endangered all that James Wright stood for.

Even though the struggle for power after 1767 consumed much of the time and energy of Governor Wright and the Assembly, the business of government went on its routine way. There were still taxes to be raised, roads to be kept up, Indians to be dealt with, trade to be regulated, and a thousand and one other things for the Governor and Assembly to attend to. In addition, Governor Wright still had to dispense land, preside over his council, supervise the courts, enforce the laws, and keep an eye on the day-to-day affairs of the colony. And political questions in general, as interesting and vital as they became during these years, were by no means the main preoccupation of the colony. Rather, the colony gave itself over to enjoying and promoting the great material expansion which seemed ever to accelerate no matter what Governor Wright and the legislature did or did not do in Savannah. Every year more people came in, more slaves were bought, more land cleared, more houses built and more crops planted. Every year more rice was cultivated, more timber cut, more livestock raised. And commerce kept the pace. Governor Wright declared that Georgia at this time was the most flourishing province in America.[5] The rebel George Walton was certain that its progress in this decade was unequaled anywhere else in the entire world.[6] And the loyalist Anthony Stokes went even further to assert that no other people in all of history had experienced the rapid growth that the colonists of Georgia did under the direction of James Wright.[7]

Yet, as the political conflict intensified and deepened it engrossed more and more the time and thoughts of men of affairs and of the common folk as well. By 1774-75 politics had been reduced to a simple struggle for control, a struggle between the Royal Governor and the radicals of the Liberty party, with the decision as to whether or not Georgia would join her sister colonies in defying Britain hinging on the outcome. Business and agriculture became so intimately involved that in 1775 buying and selling, cultivating and harvesting, became secondary to politics. Political power became more important to the merchants and planters than customers and crops, for the control of the one meant enjoying the profits of the other. As a Savannah merchant ruefully put it, "Mens minds at present are not bent on Business."[8] Men knew at last that the future of their business, and of a great deal more, rested upon the

5. Wright to Board of Trade, June 8, 1768, unpub. Col. Records, XXVIII, Part 2, 560-77.
6. "Observations of the Delegates of Georgia," Jan. 10, 1781, George Walton Papers, Duke University Library.
7. Stokes, *A View of the Constitution of the British Colonies*, 115.
8. Joseph Clay to Bright & Pechin, June 10, 1775, Letter Book of Joseph Clay & Co., Ga. Hist. Soc.

outcome of the struggle between Governor Wright and the revolutionists.

The House of Assembly's message to Governor Wright in February 1767 declining to implement the Quartering Act in Georgia was the opening shot in its bid for a greater share of power. The easy if temporary victory over Wright on this point made the Liberty faction in the Assembly reckless. For the next month, it proceeded to seize every opportunity to contest, at least indirectly, the right of Parliament to impose its laws on the colony, to defy the Governor, and to deny the Council many of its traditional rights and powers. Here are revealed the two basic drives behind the opposition with which Wright had to contend: the aggrandizement of the power of the House of Assembly, and opposition to British policy. In the minds of some, the first was important mainly because it made the second possible; but these radicals were to find it no easy thing to translate the Assembly's ambitions into defiance of Great Britain. Nevertheless this was the pattern which the colonial Assembly thereafter followed in promoting its claims. Along these lines the House of Assembly at times advanced boldly. At other times it drew back, became cautious and prudent, but only to await a more opportune moment for thrusting the colony once again into bitter controversy.

The Council sitting as the upper house of the legislature was fated to bear the brunt of the Assembly's sudden onslaught in March 1767. Parliament was the ultimate target perhaps, but the awesome might of the British government was not to be challenged lightly. Where gratitude and habitual loyalty did not suffice, the realization of the colony's dependence on British support for its safety and its well-being made the House of Assembly go slow in giving offense to the home government. As for Wright, constitutionally his position as colonial governor was virtually impregnable. The opposition of the Assembly abridged his power by its very existence, but the House of Assembly could not legally deny or forceably usurp his assigned functions. His prerogatives and duties were too clearly defined and too strongly supported by the British government to admit of this, and his personal prestige and influence had by no means been dissipated by the unfortunate turn of events. But the Achilles' heel of the governor was the Council, the mainstay of his power within the colony.

There were a number of things that made the Council peculiarly vulnerable. From the beginning it had been, in theory, the equal of the lower house of the legislature; but, in actual fact, the House of Assembly had initiated most legislation, while the upper house had been content to exercise its privilege of review and amendment. It was but a step, and a short one, for the Assembly to deny once and for all the Council's right to initiate any legislation whatsoever. And the possibility of by-passing the Council altogether on controversial issues by the adoption of House resolutions in the place of introducing regular legislation suggested a fertile field for experiment. There was also at hand a precedent for loosening the Council's hold on the disbursement of public funds: the Council in South Carolina had no such power. The Council in Georgia was handicapped in dealing with the Assembly because the political base of its members, despite the prestige of their office, was not as firm as it might have been. Although the councilor was a royal official, he was at the same time an integral part of colonial society, which laid him open to local pressures and often made him the object of his countrymen's resentment. But if the Council was the weak point in Governor Wright's armor he, contrariwise, was its greatest strength. So convinced was Wright of the Council's absolute importance to him that he was always ready to throw his considerable weight on the Council's side in any altercation with the lower house.

The Assembly's attempted raid on the Council's powers in March 1767 grew out of a dispute over the election of an agent for the colony. After the initial appointment of William Knox in 1761, Georgia, like the other American colonies, had had an agent in England to represent its interests there. The procedure for Knox's annual reappointment had heretofore been for the lower house each year to introduce and adopt an ordinance for his election, for the Council to approve the ordinance, and for the governor to give it his consent. Knox's instructions had come from a committee composed of at least two councilors and three or more assemblymen, called the committee of correspondence. In the fall of 1765, when the infuriated Assembly had suspended Knox for his support of the Stamp Act, the Council had refused to go along, even though Governor Wright indirectly condoned the suspension. The House had then independently asked Charles Garth, agent for South Carolina, to act for Georgia during the remainder of Knox's term. This was the state of affairs when the legislature met in the fall of 1766.[9] One of the first things the House of Assembly did was to secure an advance of £154 from the treasurer for Garth's past year's salary, which it ordered to be paid him. Later in the session, early in March, the Assembly sent the Council an ordinance making Garth the regular agent for the next year. Arguing the unsuitability of one man's representing the interests of both South Carolina and Georgia, the Council promptly set the ordinance aside.

Upon receiving the annual tax bill about one week later, the members of the Council found occasion to air their resentment at the Assembly's handling of the Garth affair. They were incensed to discover that £154 had been designated to repay the treasurer for his advance on Garth's salary. When the Council asked for a conference on the bill, the lower house refused, maintaining that money bills were sent up to it solely for its approval or rejection. The Council's complaint was that in the dealings with Garth its right to share in all legislation and to supervise the payment of the public accounts had been completely ignored: it had had no part in hiring Garth; it had not agreed to pay his salary; and the money for his salary had

9. Habersham to Samuel Lloyd, Sept. 5, 1767, Ga. Hist. Soc., *Colls.*, VI, 58-60.

been paid out without its approval. Because of the importance of the tax bill, the Council did pass it, but reluctantly and only after entering a strenuous protest at the highhanded actions of the Assembly.[10]

The disagreement over the appointment of Garth further complicated relations between the two houses. Despite the increase in population and trade, the £7410 issued in 1761 was still the only authorized Georgia paper currency which was legal tender. In response to a demand from the merchants of the colony, the two houses agreed to petition the King and Parliament for permission to triple this amount. But the Council balked at having Garth present the petitions, and the matter was dropped.[11] In the meantime, the House of Assembly was throwing its weight around in other ways. Wright was hard put to prevent the House from cutting important items out of the estimate sent down by the Governor in Council. Two bills for establishing ferries were dropped when the Assembly refused to accept Council amendments designed to bring the bills into line with British law.[12] Contrary to established practice, the Assembly sent up a bill for erecting a lazaretto on Tybee Island with the names in the list of commissioners all filled, leaving no blanks for the Council. It attempted to prevent the Council's inserting the names of its nominees on the grounds that this was a money bill, a distinction usually applied in the past only to the general tax bill.[13] Thus, in one way or another, the Assembly harassed the Council all during the month of March; and, as the session drew near an end, the lower house prepared a final push.

10. Journal of Assembly, Nov. 10, 1766, Jan. 14, Mar. 10, 1767, *Col. Records,* XIV, 387, 407, 458; Journal of Upper House, Mar. 12, 18-20, 1767, *ibid.,* XVII, 356, 362-68.

11. Journal of Assembly, Feb. 4, 10, 1767, *ibid.,* XIV, 427-28, 431-32; Journal of Upper House, Feb. 4, 10-11, 17, Mar. 19-20, 1767, *ibid.,* XVII, 321-23, 327-30, 332-33, 363-71.

12. Wright to Shelburne, Apr. 6, 1767, unpub. Col. Records, XXXVII, 177-90; Journal of Upper House, Feb. 19, 1767, *Col. Records,* XVII, 334-35.

13. Journal of Upper House, Mar. 6, 1767, *Col. Records,* XVII, 342-43; Journal of Assembly, Mar. 11, 1767, *ibid.,* XIV, 459.

The session ended March 26, and on that day the Assembly struck on all fronts. In the morning, it settled the business of providing an agent for the colony in short order: Garth was to be the agent; a committee of assemblymen was to correspond with him; the committee was to pay Garth as soon as he accepted the appointment; the petitions for a new issue of currency were to come from the House of Assembly alone; and Garth was to present the petitions to the King and Parliament.[14]

While making arrangements for its private agent, the House got word that during the morning Governor Wright had received instructions to disband at once the colony's Rangers. Fifteen or twenty royal troopers would remain at Augusta and a half dozen to the south at Frederica, but the dispersal of the Rangers would leave unmanned Fort George on Cockspur Island at the mouth of the Savannah River. Wright, calling the members of the Assembly up to the council chamber, urged them to make temporary provision for keeping men there to enforce the laws of trade while he pleaded with General Gage for additional soldiers. He also recommended that they reconsider the stand they had taken earlier on the Quartering Act.

The House of Assembly was in a predicament. It had already gone on record as being unwilling to appropriate the one hundred or so pounds required by the Quartering Act to purchase provisions for the royal troops stationed at Augusta and Frederica. Now, with the Rangers disbanded, the assemblymen, like Wright, were anxious not only to keep these thirty-odd men but also to have General Gage send more to Georgia. In order to avoid offending Gage and yet avoid the appearance of complying with the Quartering Act, the House directed a resolution to Governor Wright authorizing him to pay each royal officer and soldier stationed in the colony a certain amount per day. Wright reminded the Assembly that votes of credit could not be paid out until both houses had requested the Governor to order the treasurer to do so. Defiantly, the lower house did exactly

14. *Col. Records*, XIV, 469-74.

what he had said it could not do. It ordered the treasurer to make available nearly £200 for the support of a company of royal troops should General Gage see fit to send one. By specifying that the money should be paid to the men instead of going for supplies as the Act required, the House again avoided any appearance of obeying the Quartering Act. Then it voted down a motion that the order be sent up to the Council for its approval. When the House returned to the council chamber in the late afternoon, Governor Wright once more rebuked it for not complying with the Quartering Act, but he signed the prepared bills and then adjourned the General Assembly until the next fall.[15]

Wright was perturbed but undismayed in the spring and summer of 1767 as he reviewed the actions of the Commons House of Assembly in the past session.[16] Its antics had confirmed him in his belief that the outright repeal of the Stamp Act had been a calamity. "The Sovreignty of Great Britain in America has reced such a wound as I doubt it will scarce ever recover," he wrote after the legislature had adjourned, and "acts of the British Parliament will I fear for the Future, have very little weight in America." And it seemed to him that the conduct of the Assembly leaders made it "too evident that their Views were, & are, to thwart the Sovreignity of Great Britain, to destroy or weaken the weight of the Council as an Upper House, and to Endeavour to assume to themselves unproper Powers." The greatest threat lay, he believed, in the Assembly's encroachment on the prerogatives of the Council. If allowed to go unchecked, it would, he feared, have the most pernicious consequences. "In a very little time," the Assembly would "take to themselves every kind of Power, make Cyphers of the Council & in some degree of His Majesties Governors

15. Journal of Assembly, Mar. 26, 1767, Jan. 29, Feb. 2, 1768, *ibid.*, 469-78, 509-12, 513-24; Wright to Shelburne, Apr. 6, 1767, unpub. Col. Records, XXXVII, 177-90; Wright to Gage, Apr. 2, July 20, 1767, Gage Papers, Clements Lib.

16. See Wright's letters in unpub. Col. Records, XXXVII, 177-90, 215-27, 240-52, 256-57; XXVIII, Part 2, 481, 495-507.

too."[17]   As an effective check, Wright strongly and repeatedly urged the government in London to refuse to recognize Garth as provincial agent.   If this were done, and if the Governor were "authorized in His Majesties Name to Require a literal Compliance with the Terms of the Mutiny Act, and to declare to the Assembly his Majesties disapprobation of their Conduct," Wright felt "Pretty certain" that he would be able to "reduce them into Proper Bounds."[18]

Wright's confidence in his ability to control the Assembly if supported by the British government was based on a shrewd estimate of the general state of mind in the lower house of the legislature.   He realized that the men in the Assembly of Georgia were just beginning to ape "their Republican Spirited Neighbors" in South Carolina.[19]   Having meekly let Governor Wright lead them by the nose in the Stamp Act days, the assemblymen were bent upon cutting a better figure in 1767. Wright also knew that most of the men in the Assembly would go along with the leaders of the Liberty faction in badgering the provincial Council and governor but would stick at standing up to the British government.   The least threat of the withdrawal of British support, Wright calculated, would give pause to all but the most rabid Liberty Boys, making it possible for the Governor and his supporters to enlist the aid of the moderates in checkmating the radical leaders of the Liberty party.

Armed with assurance of full backing from home, Governor Wright called the legislature together in the fall of 1767 and demanded in the name of the King that the Assembly comply with the terms of the Quartering Act.   The House submissively promised to provide the required money for supplies and also agreed to pay for the troops which Governor Wright had kept at Cockspur during the summer.   But at the same time it appointed a committee to make a report which would show that

17. Wright to Shelburne, Apr. 6, 1767, *ibid.*, XXXVII, 177-90.
18. Wright to Board of Trade, June 15, 1767, *ibid.*, XXVIII, Part 2, 495-507.
19. *Ibid.*; Wright to Gage, Dec. 1, 1767, Gage Papers, Clements Lib.

it had in fact provided the required funds on the last day of the previous session. After congratulating the House of Assembly on showing a proper spirit, Governor Wright immediately adjourned the legislature until the "fever" which was raging in the lowcountry had abated.[20]

When the legislature reconvened on January 11, 1768, the House of Assembly was in full retreat from the position it had taken a year before. The only question now was how best to save face and minimize the political capital which the Governor and Council would make out of the rout. The first move of the House was to draw up an address to Governor Wright. The address, in a way absurd, was rather effective. Gone were the truculent, proud words of the previous winter. The House had become all injured innocence. The Commons House of Assembly, it seems, had never attempted to curtail the powers of the Council or to usurp its functions. On the contrary, the lower house had been left no choice but to act alone when the Council refused to cooperate. Far from disobeying the Quartering Act, the House had given Wright twice as much money for British troops as the provisions required by the Act would have cost. In fact, Governor Wright, it declared, was to blame for the whole miserable situation. Not only had he given the Board of Trade a false impression of the actions and motives of the men in the Georgia Assembly, but he also had done the entire colony a disservice by imputing to its elected representatives a disloyalty which they did not feel. The address made no mention of great principles, of the rights of the colonists, of the injustice of Parliament's tax laws. The House of Assembly had shifted ground. From challenging the constitutional position of the royal governor and his council and balking at obeying the laws of Parliament, it had turned to a less risky attack on the person of James Wright. After closing the address with a supercilious reference to Wright's love and knowl-

20. Journal of Assembly, Oct. 27-30, 1767, *Col. Records*, XIV, 479-89; Wright to Shelburne, Oct. 31, 1767, unpub. Col. Records, XXXVII, 264.

edge of the law, the members of the lower house of the legislature sat back to await the Governor's reaction.[21]

Governor Wright delayed for three days his answer to this extraordinary address from the Assembly. Then on February 2 Wright, face to face with the Assembly, forgot his uncharacteristic resolve "not to enter into any altrecation with the House." In an angry and verbose message characterized by labored sarcasm and superfluous self-righteous recrimination, he reviewed in detail its activities of the past March. He began by castigating the assemblymen for their disobedient and disrespectful attitude in refusing to provide the supplies required by the Quartering Act. He followed this up by informing them that he was well aware of their attempts to make "Cyphers of the Council" and made it plain that he would not countenance it. As for their "Mock Agent," Wright promised that if his influence would effect it, Garth would not be received by any official in London. After a scornful allusion to the personal "insinuations" in the Assembly's address, Wright ended his summary with a blunt and harsh command that the House "forthwith" comply with the King's orders to implement the Quartering Act in Georgia. He left the Assembly no loophole whereby it could avoid making its compliance with the Act appear to be anything but abject surrender to the Governor. Since the bitter pill had to be swallowed, a thin coating was devised: the Assembly ignored Wright's demand for a separate bill and instead included the required appropriation in the general tax bill for the year.[22]

When British officialdom refused to recognize Garth, the colony was left without an agent in London. The Assembly decided in late January 1768 to send up to the Council a regular ordinance for appointing Garth. This was done, the Assembly asserted, "to Accommodate any difference subsisting between

21. Journal of Assembly, Jan. 29, 1768, *Col. Records*, XIV, 509-12.
22. *Ibid.*, 513-23; Wright to Board of Trade, June 8, 1768, unpub. Col. Records, XXVIII, Part 2, 560-77.

the Two Houses" and "not from a Conviction of any Error" in the past.[23] The Council wasted no time in turning the ordinance down. The same objections to Garth still existed that had a year before. Denied even a partial victory, the Assembly again gave in to the Council. Because of "an absolute necessity to appoint an Agent," it recommended Benjamin Franklin whom the Council accepted without enthusiasm.[24] The Assembly's surrender both on the Quartering Act and on the appointment of an agent was opposed in the House by diehards among the Liberty men; but the two ferry bills were quietly altered to remove the Council's objections.[25] This done, the Assembly had backed down on every one of its claims of 1767. Filled with satisfaction, Governor Wright appeared before the General Assembly on April 11, 1768, and dissolved it at the request of the House.

The first stage of the struggle between the Governor and the Assembly was over, and Governor Wright had emerged apparently unscathed. The powers and prerogatives of his royal office had proved superior to the pretensions of the popular assembly, his skill as a politician at least equal to that of the radicals who opposed him. But there was enough in the situation in 1768 to give Wright pause. The contrast between the assemblymen of 1764 who were eagerly cooperative, almost fawning, and these same men in 1767-68 who were at first defiant, on the attack, and then at the end subdued but resentful, reveals how far Georgia had traveled in four years. And it boded no good for the future. Britain and her American colonies were still at cross-purposes; Georgia was one of those colonies. In the years to follow, Governor Wright was to be called upon again and again to defend his office and his government against the onslaughts of the House of Assembly. The

23. Journal of Assembly, Feb. 3, 1768, *Col. Records*, XIV, 525-26.
24. Journal of Assembly, Mar. 15, 1768, *ibid.*, 567; Ga. Hist. Soc., *Colls.*, VI, 64-65.
25. Journal of Assembly, Mar. 10, 1768, *Col. Records*, XIV, 565.

specific issues changed, but the general lines of attack and the outcome were the same, until the radicals changed the mode and locale of their operations from a conventional bid for power within the established colonial legislature to an extralegal and revolutionary bid outside it.

CHAPTER VII

Governor Wright and the House of Assembly: The Stalemate, 1768-1774

GOVERNOR WRIGHT almost immediately got proof that his rout of the Assembly in 1767-68 had not laid to rest the trouble from that quarter, but that instead it was only the opening chapter in a long and tiresome tale. On the same day that he dissolved the Assembly in April 1768, he ordered writs for forming a new one.[1] The ensuing election, which began on May 2 at Savannah, was the pivotal one held in Georgia before the Revolution.[2] Governor Wright and the Liberty party submitted their respective cases to the freeholders; it was their one real trial of strength at the polls.

Getting off to a convivial start at a meeting of the Union Society at Savannah on April 23, the Sons of Liberty waged a campaign as significant as it was effective.[3] They based their bid for control of the House of Assembly on the "heretical" argument that there was "a distinction between the Interest of the People & the Interest of the Crown & Mother Country." To persuade the voters of this conflict of interests, the Liberty people made many charges: that the Stamp Act was to be revived, that a court of exchequer was to be set up in Georgia, that Parliament planned to fetter the colony with other and harsher laws. The governor and the royal officials of the

1. Minutes of Gov. and Council, Apr. 11, 1768, *Col. Records*, X, 474.
2. *Ga. Gaz.*, May 4, 1768; *S. C. Gaz.*, May 16, 1768.
3. *Ga. Gaz.*, Apr. 20, 27, 1768.

colony, including the Council, it was maintained, were bound to enforce any and all of these oppressive measures. None but representatives elected by the colonists themselves and dedicated to the cause of Liberty could be counted upon to "protect & secure them in the enjoyment of their Liberty & Property." The freeholders could recognize a friend of Liberty by the stand he had taken against the Stamp Act in 1765-66. Those who had supported Wright in its enforcement were the enemies of the people and had to be everywhere opposed and rooted out. The Townshend Acts enacted in the fall of 1767, though not yet the cause of widespread resentment in America, certainly lent force to these arguments.[4]

Excitement ran high at the polls; armed men appeared and mobs formed. As poll after poll was taken on successive days throughout the province, it became apparent that the victory of the Liberty party was overwhelming. Nearly two thirds of the old members were re-elected; eighteen of the twenty-five representatives chosen were avowed Sons of Liberty. Of these, Noble Wimberly Jones, Archibald Bulloch, William Ewen, William Young, Edward Telfair, and John Smith were to become leaders of the revolutionary movement in 1774-75. In fact, more than half the membership of this House was to sit in the provincial congress which in July 1775 organized power for the revolutionists. Jones, the son of the old councilor Noble Jones and always a leading light in the Liberty faction, was unopposed for the speakership. So decisive was the vote for the Liberty candidates in 1768, particularly at and about Savannah, that Governor Wright and his supporters did not often bother thereafter to enter candidates in the elections.[5] Whatever amount of tory sentiment there may have been in the merchant-planter class of Georgia before the Revolution,

4. Wright to Hillsborough, May 23, 31, 30, 1768, unpub. Col. Records, XXXVII, 274-92, 311-13, 305-7; Wright to Board of Trade, June 8, 1768, *ibid.*, XXVIII, Part 2, 560-77.

5. *Ga. Gaz.*, July 6, 1768; *S. C. Gaz.*, May 16, 1768; Wright to Hillsborough, May 23, 1768, unpub. Col. Records, XXXVII, 274-92.

"the Lower Sort of People," as Wright called them, demonstrated at the polls that by this time they were already pretty solidly on the side of "Liberty."[6]

The issues brought out in the campaign helped to make clear the opposing principles from which the Governor and the Commons House of Assembly viewed the government of the colony and its proper relationship to the mother country. The Assembly emerged from the election as the champion for the colonists against any attempts, real or imaginary, of the Governor and Council to further the interests of Britain at the expense of the colonies. Governor Wright and his followers, standing pat on the dictum that "the Interests of Great Britain and the Colonies are one and the same," affirmed their belief in the policy of obedience to the laws of Parliament as the only way to assure that Georgia would continue to enjoy the support and protection of the mother country.[7] The line was being drawn.

Governor Wright refused to admit surprise or particular disappointment at the defeat of his followers and the decisive victory of the Liberty party in the elections. He chose rather to attribute the outcome almost entirely to the success with which "a few turbulent factious & seditious People" had stirred up the passions of the voters, passions already aroused by the inflammatory writings being sent to the colony from the northward.[8] As soon as the excitement over the election had subsided, Governor Wright set about reinforcing his position for the coming contest with the lower house. A political realist, he evidently now reconciled himself to the prospect of being saddled indefinitely with an aggressively competitive Assembly. And it was just as well he did. The Liberty party's demonstration of strength at the polls made it inevitable that its leaders

6. Wright to Hillsborough, Dec. 26, 1768, unpub. Col. Records, XXVIII, Part 2, 681-88; Habersham to Wright, Feb. 17, 1772, Ga. Hist. Soc., *Colls.*, VI, 165-67.

7. Journal of Assembly, Oct. 21, 1767, *Col. Records*, XIV, 486-89.

8. Wright to Hillsborough, May 23, 30, 1768, unpub. Col. Records, XXXVII, 274-92, 305-7.

in the Assembly should soon launch a new attack upon Governor Wright and again seek to extend the powers of the House at his expense.

In preparing for the anticipated struggle with the legislature, Governor Wright attempted to follow up the advantage which the backing of the home government had given him in the last session of the old Assembly. He particularly wished support for further restrictions on the House of Assembly's right to make appropriations. Fearing that the rock upon which the new legislature would split was the Council's continued refusal to approve the £154 paid to Garth by the lower house two years before, Governor Wright asked the Board of Trade for explicit approval of the Council's stand. Much to Wright's surprise and pleasure, the leaders of the Liberty party in the Assembly came to him shortly after the election and settled the dispute over Garth's salary to everyone's satisfaction, thus removing the last outstanding point of disagreement between the two houses several months before the new legislature convened at Savannah.[9]

The session which began November 15, 1768, was at the outset marked by "the greatest harmony possible between the three Branches of the Legislature."[10] But trouble was brewing. Opposition to the Townshend Acts had been rising in America, and in the late summer the speaker of the old Assembly, Alexander Wylly, at this time certainly one of the Sons of Liberty, had received two circular letters, one from the General Court of Massachusetts and one from the Virginia House of Burgesses, both protesting the Townshend Acts on the grounds that Parliament could not rightfully tax the colonists who were not and could not be represented in the British legislature. Having read in the August 31 issue of the *Gazette* Wylly's reply to the Massachusetts speaker promising that the Georgia

9. Wright to Board of Trade, June 8, 1768, *ibid.*, XXVIII, Part 2, 560-77.
10. Wright to Hillsborough, Dec. 24, 1768, *ibid.*, XXXVII, 380-81.

Assembly would consider the letter when it met in the fall, Governor Wright warned the Assembly at the opening of the session that any notice taken of the circular letters would be good and sufficient reason for immediate dissolution. Convinced from his private conversations with several of the leaders of the House that his warning had had the desired effect, Wright was lulled into a false sense of security which allowed the Assembly to catch him off guard.

On the day before Christmas, at one o'clock in the afternoon, the speaker, Noble Wimberly Jones, requested the Governor to give his assent to the bills already passed and then to adjourn the House until January 9. On being told that the bills would be ready for his signature at six o'clock, Wright invited the Assembly to come at that time to the council chamber. Apparently he failed to see in the unprecedented passage of the tax bill before the Christmas recess a hint that something was afoot. At five o'clock, the House produced and quickly adopted an address to the King similar in tone and content to the Massachusetts and Virginia circular letters. When Governor Wright came into the council chamber at six, the clerk of the Assembly rushed upstairs to tell him of what was going on down on the floor of the House. So well-laid and well-timed were the plans that before Wright could dissolve the Assembly, the damage had been done. Deciding to salvage what he could from the session, he called the House up to the council chamber, gave his assent to the prepared bills, ridiculed the talk of duties to regulate trade as opposed to duties for revenue as a "Distinction without a Difference," and only then dissolved the Assembly.[11]

During the winter and spring of 1768, James Wright's thinking on the long and bitter quarrel between Britain and her

11. Journal of Assembly, Dec. 24, 1768, *Col. Records*, XIV, 640-59; Journal of Upper House, Nov. 15, 1768, *ibid.*, XVII, 452-54; *Ga. Gaz.*, Dec. 28, 1768; *S. C. Gaz.*, Jan. 5, 1769; Wright to Hillsborough, Dec. 24, 1768, unpub. Col. Records, XXXVII, 380-81; Wright to Board of Trade, Nov. 18, 1768, *ibid.*, 384-86.

American colonies underwent a fundamental change.[12]   From the days of the colonial defiance of the Stamp Act, he had held that it was urgent that the colonists be forced, by harsh means if necessary, to submit to the authority of the British government. Not satisfied that the Declaratory Act was sufficient, he had wished for another blunt statement from a united Parliament, endorsed by the King, reasserting the absolute sovereignty of the British Parliament over the American colonies.   The sovereignty of Parliament could be re-established, Wright had firmly believed, only if the British government enforced a law taxing the colonists, the point at which the colonies most violently attacked the supremacy of the British legislature.   Such a law could be enforced, he had steadfastly maintained, if sufficient troops were stationed in each province to uphold the hand of the governor against the mobs.   Given sufficient force (to Wright's mind the key to the success of British policy), the governor could make examples of any person or group who dared defy the tax law.   If this were done, and done with due promptness and severity, the supremacy of Parliament would not again soon be challenged.   Amity between the chastened colonies and the mother country would at last be restored.

Observing the growing storm of resentment at the Townshend Acts and weighing what he knew of the character and temper of the Americans in the summer of 1769, James Wright decided that it was too late for any of these things to do any good—too late for an assertion of Parliament's unlimited sovereignty, too late to send troops, too late to enforce a token tax law, even too late *not* to enforce the law as long as the *right* to pass such a law was maintained.   Although neither at this nor at a later time did Wright ever for a moment question Parliament's "absolute Right to bind the Colonies" in "all cases whatever," he suggested in August 1769 that a new line

12. Wright's views on this question are brought out in many of his letters, but in Wright to Hillsborough, Aug. 15, 1769, in unpub. Col. Records, XXXVII, 409-13, he reviews the opinions he has held in the past and gives his new ideas on the subject.

be drawn, that the constitution be changed so as to satisfy the claims of the colonists.[13]   Until Parliament had renounced its right to levy taxes in America, Wright saw no hope of a settlement ever being reached.   This was a momentous, not to say shattering, decision for an old tory like Wright.   The fact that a man of his deep conservatism and stubborn temperament should make so great a concession to expediency gives some idea how great and how dark the shadow over the old Empire had grown.   It also reveals, as events were to show, how keen an insight James Wright had into the American situation in 1769. And once he had accepted the necessity of appeasing the colonists, Wright never left off urging his government "to settle the line with respect to *Taxation &c* by some new mode or Constitution."[14]

Governor Wright, who had reported to Lord Hillsborough the details of the Assembly's Christmas Eve coup, got instructions from him on June 19, 1769, to issue writs for a new House of Assembly at the first favorable moment.[15]   But before the new House met in the fall, Governor Wright was again cast down by local reverberations arising from agitations up the coast where the other American colonies were entering upon nonimportation agreements to force the repeal of the Townshend duties.   In September, several meetings were held in Savannah for the purpose of preparing resolutions which it was hoped would align Georgia with her sister colonies.   The guiding spirit in the resolution-making was Jonathan Bryan, a great planter and long-time councilor who broke with his fellow members.   He got himself expelled for his trouble and became one of Wright's most influential opponents in the troublous days ahead.   Most of the local merchants and planters did not share Bryan's enthusiasm for economic retaliation, and the meetings

13. *Ibid.*
14. Wright to Dartmouth, Aug. 24, 1774, Ga. Hist. Soc., *Colls.*, III, 180-82.
15. Hillsborough to Wright, Mar. 23, 1769, unpub. Col. Records, XXXVII, 394-97.

aroused little excitement.[16]   Taking the position that his disapproval would be more a spur than a hindrance, Governor Wright pursued a hands-off policy.[17]   Long before the new Assembly came to Savannah, the radicals had given up any hope of closing the ports of Georgia.   One Son of Liberty, Edward Telfair, consoled himself with the pleasing prospect of Savannah's getting "a good lift" by becoming "a principal Export for Carolina produce" once the port of Charleston was closed.[18]

The new Assembly met at Savannah on October 30, 1769. After agreeing with the sentiments of a resolution of the dissolved Virginia House of Burgesses that the burgesses, and the burgesses alone, had the right to tax the people of Virginia, the Assembly seemed satisfied that it had sufficiently asserted itself, and without further ado settled down to business.   The session promised to be a harmonious one.[19]   Tensions were eased by the report that the Townshend tax on glass, paper, and paint was to be repealed and no new duties imposed.[20]   Pleased by the success of his policy of ignoring the nonimportation resolutions, Governor Wright had less inclination than usual to stir up trouble.[21]   The new Assembly, which lacked the poise and finesse that former assemblies had evinced in their dealings with the Governor, was slow to act.   The majority of the members were new, many old ones having retired after serving continuously from 1764.   But back were such old hands—and Liberty leaders—as John Milledge, Archibald Bulloch, William Young, William Ewen, and Noble Wimberly Jones, while among the new members were Button Gwinnett, Samuel Elbert,

16. *Ga. Gaz.*, Sept. 6, 13, 20, Oct. 4, 1769; *S. C. Gaz.*, Mar. 15, 1770.

17. Wright to Hillsborough, Sept. 20, 1769, May 10, 1770, unpub. Col. Records, XXXVII, 417-18, 441-42.

18. Edward Telfair to Basil Cowper, Oct. 7, 1769, Telfair Papers, Duke. Telfair's relationship to the Liberty party was equivocal, but in the end he became a leader of the Revolution in Georgia.

19. Journal of Assembly, Nov. 7, 1769, *Col. Records*, XV, 31-33; Wright to Hillsborough, Nov. 8, 1769, unpub. Col. Records, XXXVII, 423.

20. Benjamin Franklin to Noble W. Jones, Apr. 3, June 7, 1769, in Journal of Assembly, Nov. 7, 1769, *Col. Records*, XV, 26-30.

21. Wright to Hillsborough, Nov. 8, Sept. 20, 1769, unpub. Col. Records, XXXVII, 423, 417-18.

and Benjamin Andrew, all destined to become Revolutionary leaders. Perhaps partly because of the members' inexperience in conducting public affairs and partly, Wright maintained, because of the machinations of three new members who had hit upon the technique of deliberately obstructing all public business in order to harass the Governor, the session dragged on for month after month.[22]

During this session, which lasted until May 1770, Governor Wright was given little trouble; but the House made it clear in two instances that it had not abandoned the stance assumed by its predecessor. For five years the legislature of Georgia had been trying to frame a bill for governing Negroes which would meet with the approval of the British government. The long delay in putting this and other necessary legislation into effect, because it had to be reviewed and approved in London, had become exceedingly irksome. In this session, the House passed a Negro bill without the required suspending clause and sent it up to the Council. When it became apparent that the Council was not going to pass the bill without the usual clause, the Assembly agreed to its insertion but, significantly, "solely from the Necessity of the Case, and not from any Conviction that such a Clause ought to be inserted in any Bill whatsoever."[23]

The second instance of the temper of the generally quiescent House was in the end more serious. It brought the Assembly into collision with the Governor and set off a train of events which eventually resulted in repeated dissolutions of the Commons House and a prolonged interruption of public business. In November the House suddenly woke up to the fact that for years it had been doing in the colony just what it had denied the right of Parliament to do in America. The legislature of Georgia had been taxing the people of four southern parishes, none of which was represented in the Assembly. The House demanded that the unrepresented parishes be given seats

22. Wright to Hillsborough, May 11, 1770, *ibid.*, 443-48.
23. Journal of Assembly, Mar. 14, 1770, *Col. Records*, XV, 152.

immediately.   Unappeased by Wright's repeated insistence that
he could not issue writs of elections in these parishes until he had
got permission from London, the Assembly threatened to delay
the general tax bill until the southern parishes were represented.
When it did finally pass the tax bill in March 1770, the House
exempted the inhabitants of the unrepresented parishes.[24]   Although Governor Wright was incensed at the Assembly's threat
to hold up legislation until its demands were met, he wrote
for permission to issue the election writs as soon as the necessary
petitions were in.[25]

On the whole, Governor Wright was satisfied with the
work of the session of 1769-70.   When he called the Assembly
back to Savannah in the fall of 1770 he expected no trouble,
unless his inability to permit the elections in the four southern
parishes should upset the assemblymen.[26]   The House promptly
demanded once again that writs be issued in these parishes, and
Wright again explained he could not do so.[27]   Nothing more
was said on the subject for several months; but, on February
20, 1771, the House angrily resolved for a second time not to
consider the annual tax bill until the elections were held.[28]

Clearly, Governor Wright was now contending with an
Assembly which fully understood the implications of its control of the purse strings and was determined to exploit it to the
fullest.   But here Wright's advantage was that, unlike most
royal governors, he drew funds for the royal establishment from
the British Treasury and not from colonial tax receipts.   Permission to issue the desired writs came on the day after the
Assembly had made its threat.   Wright immediately called in
the speaker of the House, Dr. Noble Wimberly Jones, and

24. Journal of Assembly, Nov. 16, 1769, Jan. 12, Feb. 20, 21, Mar. 15, 1770,
ibid., 47-49, 86-87, 123-24, 127-28, 153.
25. Wright to Hillsborough, May 11, Oct. 8, 1770, unpub. Col. Records,
XXXVII, 443-48, 483-85.
26. Wright to Hillsborough, May 11, July 20, Aug. 22, Oct. 8, 1770, Feb.
28, 1771, *ibid.*, 443-48, 464-68, 474, 483-85, 520-28; Wright to Board of
Trade, July 23, 1770, *ibid.*, XXXVIII, Part 2, 727-33.
27. Journal of Assembly, Oct. 24, 26, 1770, *Col. Records*, XV, 199-202, 206-7.
28. *Ibid.*, 298-99.

showed him the letter from Lord Hillsborough, which not only approved of elections in the southern parishes but allowed all but one of the other changes in the election law advocated by the Assembly—the House was denied the right to limit its life to three years. Spoiling for a fight, the House seized upon this as a pretext for renewing its attack upon the Governor. Instead of rescinding the resolution delaying the tax bill as Wright had expected, the members "Bellow'd on their Rights and Priv-ileges, and the Plenitude of their Powers" until the House ad-journed for the day. The next morning Governor Wright dis-solved the Assembly, and a few days later ordered new elec-tions.[29]

The dissolution of the Assembly initiated a new phase in the conflict between Wright and the Assembly. For the next two years a defiant House stood toe to toe with an adamant Gov-ernor, neither yielding an inch. The consequence was that no business was transacted by the Georgia legislature. Although there were no burning issues at stake in the Empire to give it bite and scope, the struggle for power between royal governor and popular assembly continued unabated in Georgia, and else-where. The repeal of the Townshend Acts did little to mollify an ambitious Assembly intent not only upon opposing parlia-mentary taxation but also upon gaining a position within the colony which would give it the upper hand in its dealings with the Royal Governor.

The new House convened in April 1771 a few weeks after the dissolution of the old, and unanimously re-elected Noble Wimberly Jones speaker. Wright rejected the radical Jones, and the House replaced him with Archibald Bulloch, like Jones a Son of Liberty in Savannah and later president of the Revolu-tionary government. On the next day, April 25, it adopted a resolution declaring Wright's rejection of its speaker "a high Breach of the Privilege of the House."[30] The private re-

29. Wright to Hillsborough, Feb. 28, 1771, unpub. Col. Records, XXXVII, 520-28.
30. Journal of Assembly, *Col. Records*, XV, 312.

monstrances of several members of the Council urging the
leaders of the House to withdraw the resolution being to no
avail, Governor Wright dissolved this General Assembly on
the third day of its sitting, and shortly afterwards left for his
planned visit to England.[31]

James Habersham, the president of the Council, took over
the government of the colony during Wright's absence of nearly
two years. Before sailing, Wright recommended to his old
colleague that he delay ordering new elections until he had got
official reaction to the Assembly's denial of the governor's right
to reject its speaker.[32] There was some talk among the Liberty
leaders in the Assembly of showing Habersham such deference
and support that Governor Wright's reputation would suffer by
contrast. Though anxious for cooperation, Habersham ab-
horred the thought of being used to embarrass his great friend
and mentor. He labored to avoid any appearance of coveting
Wright's office or of wishing to court popularity at the expense
of the principles for which both he and Wright stood. Old
and infirm, he had no political ambitions and genuinely longed
for Wright's return so as to be "freed from the honorable Cares
of Government."[33]

Habersham waited a full year before forming a new legislature. His instructions were to reject the first speaker presented by the House, thereby establishing the governor's right
of rejection. When a committee of the Assembly informed him
on the first day of the session, April 21, 1772, that the House
had chosen Noble Wimberly Jones, Habersham replied that he
was under the King's orders to signify his disapproval of its
choice. The House then re-elected Jones and again Habersham
rejected him, explaining that his objection to Jones was not
personal. On his being elected a third time, Jones declined

31. Journal of Assembly, Apr. 26, 1771, *ibid.*, 315; Wright to Hillsborough,
Apr. 30, 1771, unpub. Col. Records, XXXVII, 535-38.
32. Habersham to Hillsborough, Sept. 26, 1771, unpub. Col. Records, XXXVII,
554-58.
33. Habersham to Wright, May 30, 1772, Ga. Hist. Soc., *Colls.*, VI, 180-82, ff.

with the excuse that the press of his private affairs would not permit him to serve. Habersham demanded that the record of Jones's third election and of his resignation be expunged from the journals, but the House refused, and Habersham dissolved the legislature on the third day of the session.[34]

Governor Wright and President Habersham both believed that the protracted interruption of public business, which was beginning to stretch on into years, would eventually cause a revulsion in the colony against the stubbornness of the House leadership. In order to give time for this expected reaction to make itself felt at the polls, Habersham waited until December 1772 to constitute a new legislature. Many things made it likely that in the winter of 1772-73 the House of Assembly would abandon the obstructive policy of recent years and show a change of heart.[35]

By their repeated dissolutions, Wright and Habersham had made it perfectly plain that neither had the slightest intention of giving in to the House. The result was stalemate. In playing a waiting game with the lower house, the Governor had reason once again to be thankful for the enormous advantage of not being dependent upon the House for funds to support his government. Time worked against the House of Assembly, however. By December 1772, the stalemate between Governor and Assembly had deprived the colony of a legislature for nearly two years. The urgent need for legislative action was apparent, and Habersham had good reason to hope that pressure from the people was not lacking. The stalemate had, in fact, produced an impasse, and the time was ripe for a truce, a truce on terms set by the Governor.

The men elected in November and December of 1772 proved to be generally more friendly to "government" than

34. Habersham to Hillsborough, Apr. 30, 1772, unpub. Col. Records, XXXVII, 622-36; Journal of Assembly, Apr. 21-25, 1772, *Col. Records*, XV, 315-34.
35. Habersham to Wright, Dec. 4, 1772, Ga. Hist. Soc., *Colls.*, VI, 215-18; Hillsborough to Habersham, Aug. 7, 1772, unpub. Col. Records, XXXVIII, Part 1, 1-3.

any elected since 1764. There were seven or eight Sons of Liberty in the House, including Jonathan Bryan, Noble Wimberly Jones, and Archibald Bulloch, whom Habersham could expect to oppose him pretty consistently; but he could rely on nearly as many to give him their loyal support. The remainder were apparently now inclined to get on with the public business, unless some new challenge should come from Parliament or the Governor.[36] The long vacation from the strain of daily contact in the legislature had given time for tempers to cool and for personal animosities and petty irritations to heal. With Wright out of the colony, the greatest irritant had been removed, and for a time the symbol of all that frustrated and infuriated the Sons of Liberty had not been constantly before them. Except for the tax on tea, the rights and privileges of the colonists had no tangible restrictions that could be dramatically opposed. And after a bad crop in 1771, the colony was again enjoying unprecedented prosperity. By early 1773 it was clear that the temper of the House was favorable for attending to the long-neglected affairs of the colony.

When Governor Wright returned in February, he was welcomed at the landing by a committee of the House of Assembly.[37] Finding "rather a pleasing Prospect of Harmony amongst the different Branches of the Legislature,"[38] the Governor kept it in session, except for a recess at planting time, until well into September.

James Wright's personal prestige had been greatly enhanced by his visit to England. He returned to Georgia with tangible proof that he enjoyed the full confidence of the King and his ministers. The King had made him a baronet, and the rumor was that he was soon to sit on the Board of Trade. His

36. This is one of the few sessions of which voting records are included in the Journal. A study of the voting record reveals rather clearly the factional alignments in the lower house.

37. Journal of Assembly, Feb. 11, Mar. 1, 1773, *Col. Records*, XV, 384-85, 389; *S. C. Gaz.*, Mar. 1, 1773.

38. Wright to Dartmouth, Mar. 24, 1773, unpub. Col. Records, XXXVIII, Part 1, 42-45.

success in getting approval for his scheme to purchase nearly two million acres of fertile land from the Creeks and Cherokee was acclaimed by the whole colony. The accession of this new source of wealth helped to soften any feeling of rancor against Wright which time and distance had not erased. He was pleased to note in the summer of 1773 that "Confidence and Harmony" had made their appearance in Georgia politics—for the first time since 1765.[39]

From the stalemate of 1770-72 the relations between the Governor and Assembly had moved to something resembling equilibrium in 1773. But the Governor had conceded nothing, and the House of Assembly had only retreated. The wave of excitement which swept America after the closing of the port of Boston in 1774 would probably have upset the balance once again had it not been for the Indians. At the turn of the year 1773-74, the Creeks reacted to the sale of the land by murdering several white families on the northern frontier, and the colony was still in a state of fright when the news of the Boston developments came. In the summer and fall of 1774, a rash of petitions, dissents, parish meetings, and congresses broke out all over the colony protesting passage of the Coercive Acts against the colony of Massachusetts, but the uneasy feeling that the need for British support against the Indians was more important than righting the wrongs done to faraway Boston helped to dampen enthusiasm and prevent any effective action being taken. And representatives were not even sent to the First Continental Congress. His Majesty's subjects in Georgia were always at their "dutiful and loyal" best whenever the Creeks or Cherokee acted up.[40]

The January 1775 meeting of the legislature, coming at a time when a general Indian war seemed imminent, was the occasion for one final and revealing fracas between the two houses

---

39. Wright to Dartmouth, Sept. 30, 1773, *ibid.*, 96.
40. Wright to Dartmouth, Jan. 4, 31, 1774, *ibid.*, 161, 163-71; *Ga. Gaz.*, July 13, 1774, ff.

of the legislature. The cause for the dispute was once again a disagreement over the appointment of an agent for the colony. In the end, the House of Assembly appointed its own agent, Benjamin Franklin, set up its own committee to correspond with him, and independently made provisions for paying his salary.[41] The Council protested to Wright; Wright requested that British officials not recognize the Assembly's agent; and the Board of Trade promised there would be no dealings with him.[42] Things were back where they had started in 1767. The conflict between Governor and Assembly had gone full circle. Governor Wright had held the line against all pretensions of the House of Assembly for nearly a decade. But every day in 1774 and 1775 his triumph was coming to mean less and less.

The last session of Georgia's colonial legislature aptly illustrates what was happening to the Governor. The local agitation over the Boston Port Acts reached a climax in January 1775 when a meeting was called at Savannah to provide for the colony's adoption of the recommendations of the Continental Congress. Governor Wright summoned the legislature into session on the same day that the meeting was to be held in hopes of keeping the opposition leaders in the state house where, as he had again and again proved, he could call the tune or, if need be, put a stop to the proceedings. Wright's maneuver failed, and the provincial meeting was held. But its resolutions were not adopted by the colony. A new stalemate had been reached. It was, however, no longer a stalemate between the Royal Governor and the Commons House of Assembly, but one between the royal government of the colony as such and the Liberty-led opposition standing outside the government and seeking to destroy it. For eight years James Wright had succeeded in repulsing every attack of the House of

41. *Ga. Gaz.*, Jan. 26–Mar. 12, 1774. The journals of this session are not published elsewhere and they are not complete here.
42. Wright to Dartmouth, Dec. 30, 1773, Mar. 12, 1774, unpub. Col. Records, XXVIII, Part 2, 878-86, XXXVIII, Part 1, 208-9; Dartmouth to Wright, May 4, 1774, *ibid.*, 232-33.

Assembly on what he considered the prerogatives of the royal governor and his king, and in January 1775 the structure of the royal government in Georgia was still intact and virtually unchanged. But Governor Wright was soon to see the structure he had defended so long and so well become an empty shell.

CHAPTER VIII

Sir James Wright and the Liberty Boy, 1774-1775

SAVANNAH'S WELCOME for Sir James Wright on his return from England in February 1773 lacked the exuberance of the celebration of October 1754 when the first royal governor arrived. A delegation of gentlemen was on hand at the landing; Sir Patrick Houstoun's company of light infantry and Captain Samuel Elbert's grenadiers, along with several other companies of militia, were drawn up to salute the Governor as he came ashore from the scout boat which brought him across the river from Purrysburgh. That night the usual bonfires were lighted and toasts drunk. But several leading gentlemen of the town —Noble Wimberly Jones among them—were noticeably missing from the welcoming party, and this time none of the townspeople ripped the siding from the Council House to pitch onto the blazing fires.[1]

Even so, if John Reynolds had come back from England with Governor Wright in 1773, he would have found the changes in the physical aspects of the town much more striking than any alteration in the attitude of the populace. There were still sandy streets and sandy squares, still pine forests and flat marshes, but gone was the air of desolation and neglect. Instead, there was bustling activity and a look of prosperity about the place. The bumper rice crop of the past fall was keeping the merchants of Savannah busier than ever. Along the water

1. S. C. Gaz., Mar. 1, 1773; Journal of Assembly, Feb. 11, Mar. 1, 1773, Col. Records, XV, 384-85, 389.

front, the bare bluff of 1754 was now crowded with warehouses and wharves, and ships from all over the Empire were being drawn to the port by the commodities of the colony. Brick homes, churches, and public buildings had replaced many of the depressing little huts of Reynolds' time, and new structures of all sorts stood on what had before been woods or vacant squares.[2]

James Wright could take pride in the transformation in Savannah, the show window of the solid progress that had come to the colony during nearly twenty years of royal rule. He and Henry Ellis had been the moving spirits in bringing Georgia "up from mere infancy, from next to nothing, to a considerable degree of maturity and opulence."[3] No man had ever rivaled either one in importance, influence, prestige, or power. Sir James Wright was, in one way, at the peak of his career in the spring of 1773. Full recognition of his devotion and effectiveness as servant of the King had come to him. In his role of King's representative, he was in perhaps a stronger position than any other governor in America. But his position as colonial leader was another matter. Ever since the appearance of the Sons of Liberty on the stage of colonial politics, the Governor's right to be both director and leading player had been stubbornly disputed. Not a single individual to equal him in power or ability, his rival was a composite figure, the Liberty Boy, who would soon begin to transfer his political activity from the House of Assembly to private societies and provincial or parish meetings where he could act out his role of opposition away from the watchful eye of the Governor. Imperceptibly at first, and then with quickening tempo, these extralegal meetings in 1775 took over the functions of the old co-

2. De Brahm, *History of Georgia*, 36; Habersham to Hillsborough, Aug. 12, 1772, unpub. Col. Records, XXXVIII, Part 1, 4-8; Habersham to Dartmouth, Jan. 12, 1773, *ibid.*, 38-39; Wright to Dartmouth, Mar. 24, 1773, *ibid.*, 42-45; Habersham to Wright, Sept. 24, Dec. 4, 1772, Ga. Hist. Soc., *Colls.*, VI, 211-13, 215-18.

3. Governor Wright's Address to the General Assembly, Jan. 18, 1775, unpub. Col. Records, XXXVIII, Part 1, 375-79.

lonial legislature. James Wright never yielded the center of the stage in the royal government, but before the summer of 1775 was over he found he was playing to an empty house.

In July 1774, Wright's bêtes noires, the South Carolina Liberty Boys, were "very busy in Sending Hand Bills, Letters and Public Invitations &c &c to stir up the People" of Georgia against the Boston Port Act.[4] On July 20 a notice signed by Noble Wimberly Jones, Archibald Bulloch, John Houstoun, and George Walton appeared in the *Georgia Gazette* calling for all inhabitants to come to a meeting in Savannah a week later. The mass meeting held at the Vendue House on the twenty-seventh took no action except to call for another session at Savannah on August 10, this one to be made up of deputies elected by the people. Wright attributed the delay to opposition to the proposed resolutions, but the radicals maintained that action was deferred only to allow time for election of deputies in the outlying parishes. The leading radicals stayed behind after the others had left the Vendue House and appointed a committee of correspondence of thirty-one persons, headed by John Glen, to prepare for the August meeting. Governor Wright issued a proclamation a few days later condemning the doings of July 27 and forbidding the meeting set for August 10; but he failed to intimidate the Sons of Liberty, who continued to bend every effort to get the people in all parts of the colony to send deputies to Savannah. The twenty-one who showed up on the tenth abruptly shifted to a tavern where they met behind locked doors and prepared a set of resolutions strongly critical of the closing of Boston's port and asserting anew the rights of the American colonies. Although approving the resolutions unanimously, the deputies voted down a proposal that delegates be sent to the planned continental congress.[5]

Deeply disturbed by this act of defiance and by his inability

4. Wright to Dartmouth, July 25, 1774, *ibid.*, 292-94.
5. *Ga. Gaz.*, Aug. 3, 10, 17, Sept. 7, 21, 1774.

to do anything about it, Governor Wright sent Dartmouth what was both a stern warning and an anguished plea for the British government to devise a settlement of the disputes which were tearing Britain and her colonies asunder:

It is absolutely necessary that they are brought to a *Point* & Clearly Setled and Established *some how or other,* and not suffered to remain as they are. Nothing but Jealousies Rancour and ill Blood: Law & no Law, Government & no Government, Dependence and Independence . . . and everything unhinged and Running into—Confusion, so that in short a Man hardly knows what to do, or how to act and its a most Disagreeable State to one who Wishes to Support Law Government & Good order & to discharge his Duty with Honor and Integrity.[6]

He cheered up a little in the early fall when dissents to the resolutions began to pour in from all over the province.   The opponents of the radical program (probably at Wright's instigation) had got together some five or six hundred signatures of men supposedly willing to go on public record against the resolutions of the August meeting;[7] and Governor Wright expressed the belief that "the Sense of the People" in general was against a strong stand in support of Boston.[8]

Wright's good spirits were short-lived, however, for the colony was soon raised to what seemed a new "height of phrenzy."[9]   On November 23, 1774, the committee of correspondence for the Liberty faction published a copy of the nonimportation agreement adopted by the recent Continental Congress, and urged the "Freeholders, Merchants, and other Inhabitants" to send deputies to Savannah on January 15, 1775, to decide whether Georgia should join the Association or not.[10]

6. Ga. Hist. Soc., *Colls.,* III, 182.

7. *Ga. Gaz.,* Sept. 7, 1774, ff.; Wright to Gage, Nov. 4, 1774, Gage Papers, Clements Lib.; Hugh McCall, *The History of Georgia containing Brief Sketches of the Most Remarkable Events Up to the Present Day* (*1784*) (Atlanta, 1909), 273.

8. Wright to Dartmouth, Oct. 13, 1774, unpub. Col. Records, XXXVIII, Part 1, 333.

9. Wright to Dartmouth, Dec. 13, 1774, *ibid.,* 361.

10. *Ga. Gaz.,* Nov. 23, 1774.

A treaty ending hostilities with the Creeks having been signed in late October, the heated South Carolina Liberty Boys could not much longer be put off with the excuse that Georgia's laggardly pace was due to her dependence upon British troops to aid her against the Indians.[11] The Carolinians had agreed to delaying the congress until after the new year, but they made it clear that they expected Georgia to adhere to the Association by February 1, 1775.[12] Governor Wright reported the circulation of a rumor that the Carolina Liberty Boys had sworn that if Georgia "did not Accede to the Proceedings of the Continental Congress, Blood and Devastation Should Stalk thro every Corner of it."[13] The Georgia Sons of Liberty, who were being aided by their Carolina counterparts in building up sentiment for the nonimportation regulations, were optimistic about their prospects, and in December and January the people calmly chose deputies to the provincial congress.[14]

Fearful of the outcome of all this hustle and bustle in the camp of the Liberty party, Governor Wright set himself to frustrate their designs. He bemoaned the fact that he did not have two hundred soldiers and a sloop of war to keep "every thing quiet & orderly."[15] On the day the deputies met in congress at Savannah, the Governor called the legislature into session. He had hopes of withdrawing the leadership from the congress by requiring the attendance of several important deputies and of discouraging the remaining by holding over their heads the threat of action from the legislature. Wright opened the session with perhaps the finest speech of his career. It was a persuasive and impressive plea for the elected leaders

11. *S. C. Gaz.*, Oct. 3, 1774.

12. Joseph Clay & Co. to Bright & Pechin, Dec. 10, 1774, Letter Book of Joseph Clay & Co., Ga. Hist. Soc.

13. Wright to Dartmouth, Feb. 1, 1775, unpub. Col. Records, XXXVIII, Part 1, 371-74.

14. Clay & Co. to Bright & Pechin, Dec. 10, 1774, Letter Book of Joseph Clay & Co., Ga. Hist. Soc.; Wright to Dartmouth, Dec. 13, 1774, Feb. 1, 1775, unpub. Col. Records, XXXVIII, Part 1, 361, 371-74.

15. Wright to Dartmouth, Dec. 20, 1774, unpub. Col. Records, XXXVIII, Part 1, 367-68.

of Georgia not to "be led away by the voices and opinions of men of over-heated ideas," but to "consider coolly and sensibly the terrible consequences" of what they were doing. He reminded them that "where there is no law there can be no liberty," that their happiness and well-being depended upon "the due course of law and support of government." The speech, a passionate affirmation of James Wright's political philosophy, was shot through with abhorrence of anything revolutionary, natural to one who had served his King in a public capacity for more than thirty-five years. But even as he spoke, in another part of town the deputies were preparing to draft the controversial resolutions.[16]

The congress had turned out to be a great disappointment to the Liberty people. Only five of the twelve parishes had sent deputies, and some of these men had been instructed as to the exact form the resolutions should take. The congress adopted resolutions generally in line with the recommendations of the Continental Congress but set back the date for putting into effect the bans on trade. The deputies had no hope of the colony's accepting even this. The Liberty Boys had failed to arouse enthusiasm for closing the ports of the province to British goods. Most of the Savannah merchants were opposed, and the planters as a whole were unenthusiastic. The proceedings and the resolutions of the congress were not made public, and for some time it was not generally known exactly what had been done.[17]

The real reason for going ahead with the resolutions in the face of almost certain repudiation by the colony, and also one cause for the secrecy which surrounded the proceedings, was that the deputies to the congress had hit upon an expedient

16. George White, *Historical Collections of Georgia* (New York, 1854), 50-51; Wright to Dartmouth, Feb. 1, 1775, unpub. Col. Records, XXXVIII, Part 1, 371-74.

17. Extract of a letter from Georgia to a gentleman in New York, dated Feb. 18, 1775, White, *Collections,* 61; Noble W. Jones, Archibald Bulloch, John Houstoun, to the President of the Continental Congress, Apr. 6, 1775, *ibid.,* 61-63.

which they hoped would bring Georgia into the continental association despite public apathy and resistance. The scheme was to impose, at least nominally, the nonimportation agreement on the colony in the same way that the Sons of Liberty in the House of Assembly had put Georgia on record in 1768 as being opposed to the Townshend Acts. Those deputies who also held seats in the legislature carefully laid plans to present the resolutions to the House of Assembly, "who, it was hoped, would by votes in a few minutes, and before prerogative should interfere, make it the act of the whole Province." The radical assemblymen had everything "just ready to be presented, when the Governor, either treacherously informed, or shrewdly suspecting the step, put an end to the session." Wright was, in fact, fully informed of the plans, and it was because he feared that the resolutions would be adopted that he adjourned the legislature on February 10, effectively destroying any chance of Georgia's joining the Association at this time.[18]

After both the deputies to the congress and the members of the Assembly had left Savannah, the people of Georgia continued to "fluctuate between liberty and convenience," with convenience definitely in the ascendancy during the spring of 1775.[19] In fact, leaders of the Liberty faction despaired of ever swinging the pendulum in their direction. Governor Wright succeeded in suppressing the minutes of the provincial congress, and he brought pressure to bear on the men chosen to represent Georgia at the Second Continental Congress. On April 6, the three delegates, Archibald Bulloch, John Houstoun, and Noble Wimberly Jones, notified John Hancock that they would not go to Philadelphia,[20] pointing out that it would be farcical for them to pose as representatives of a province in which sentiment was running so strongly against the congress.[21]

18. *Ibid.*, 61-63; Ga. Hist. Soc., *Colls.*, III, 196-99.
19. White, *Collections*, 61-63.
20. Wright to Dartmouth, Mar. 23, 1775, unpub. Col. Records, XXXVIII, Part 1, 418-20.
21. White, *Collections*, 61-63.

This, perhaps better than anything else, indicates how reluctant the leadership in Georgia was, even as late as the spring of 1775, to take steps which might threaten the colony's advantageous relations with Britain.

Although proud of the "great Decency and Respect" shown him by the inhabitants of Georgia, Governor Wright was repeatedly upset during the spring of 1775 by neighboring Carolinians who showed neither.[22] One prominent Carolina gentleman, while on a visit to Savannah in early April, reportedly announced before a large gathering that if any blood was spilt in Massachusetts Bay his Liberty Boys would surely come and cut the throats of the craven Georgians. And the Carolinian promised to head the party. Word also came from Charleston that the general committee there had banned all trade between South Carolina and Georgia. With the prospect of having a near monopoly on the British trade, Wright and the Savannah merchants were not cast down.[23] What infuriated Wright most was the way the South Carolina Governor seemingly gave the Liberty Boys a free hand, leaving Wright to bear the brunt of resentment from the radicals of both South Carolina and Georgia.[24]

While the South Carolinians fussed and fumed and inveighed against James Wright, the Governor observed with gratification the waning fortunes of the Georgia radicals. Their only encouragement came from St. Johns parish, peopled by Congregationalists with Massachusetts antecedents. After withdrawing from the August meeting at Savannah to adopt stronger resolutions, the men of this parish, despairing of their fellow colonists, had acted on their own. Before the provincial congress met in January, they had already announced their adherence to the nonimportation association. As a matter of fact, they sent no deputies to Savannah and instead sent a

22. Wright to Dartmouth, Feb. 1, 1775, unpub. Col. Records, XXXVIII, Part 1, 371-74.
23. Wright to Dartmouth, Apr. 24, 1775, *ibid.*, 424-29.
24. Wright to Dartmouth, Feb. 1, 1775, *ibid.*, 371-74.

deputation to Charleston in an attempt to associate themselves with the South Carolina patriots. When the Georgia delegation failed to go to Philadelphia in May, St. Johns sent Dr. Lyman Hall to represent the parish.[25] Governor Wright dismissed the activities of "these Poor Insignificant Fanatic's" as the manifestations of "a strong Tincture of Republican or Oliverian Principles" still retained;[26] but there were other and good reasons for the quite sensible people of St. Johns to be so far in advance of the rest of the colony in their zeal for the American cause. The religious tie with Massachusetts increased their sympathy for Boston and their long residence in South Carolina made it natural for them to look to rabid Charleston for leadership rather than to Savannah or London. Strict church discipline, made stronger by years of dissent in a land with an established church, gave them a ready-made organization for united action. At any rate, for a few months in the winter and spring of 1775 the people of St. Johns parish were the fly in Governor Wright's ointment.

Into the general calm of Georgia, in March and April 1775, one disquieting note was injected—not new but now grown serious. The chronic shortage of currency in the colony had suddenly become critical. Strife between the colonies and Britain had so aggravated the shortage that it had begun to cripple business. The talk of stopping the overseas trade had led the merchants to place orders in Britain far beyond their current need, while the planters had held back their rice in order to profit from the expected rise in prices.[27] The consequence was that bills of any description became "so exceeding scarce" in Savannah in the spring of 1775 as "not to be had at

25. *Ga. Gaz.*, Aug. 17, Sept. 7, Dec. 14, 1774; *S. C. Gaz.*, Sept. 6, 1774, Feb. 20, 1775.
26. Wright to Dartmouth, Apr. 23, 1775, unpub. Col. Records, XXXVIII, Part 1, 424-29.
27. Joseph Clay & Co. to John Nugent, Mar. 9, 1775, Letter Book of Joseph Clay & Co., Ga. Hist. Soc.; Joseph Clay to Michael Collins, Apr. 8, 1775, *ibid.*; Cowper & Telfair to Telfair, Cowper & Telfair, June 20, 1775, Letter Book of Edward Telfair and of Cowper & Telfair, 1773-1776, Telfair Academy.

all."[28] Despite this, however, the interruption of trade in the other colonies put Georgia in a position to "reap Such Advantages" that the prosperity begun in the early 1760's continued almost unabated until ended by the rupture in the Empire in the summer and fall of 1775.[29]

Governor Wright was feeling rather easy about his province in early May 1775. His spirits had been lifted by the news that he was to be sent one hundred soldiers and a sloop of war. The fact that not enough assemblymen had answered his summons to make a House on May 9 was not too alarming; neither had the proposed provincial congress materialized on the tenth. Wright now believed that the failure of the January congress meant that nothing would ever be done about associating Georgia with the other colonies in the Continental Congress.[30] The Liberty people were inclined to agree with him.[31] However, both the Governor and the Liberty Boys were keeping anxious eyes on Massachusetts. No one was greatly surprised when on May 10 news came from Charleston of fighting between the colonists and British troops in New England, but the Liberty Boys were quick to play up the story of bloodshed. Georgia began to stir, and on the night of the eleventh several Liberty Boys, headed by Noble Wimberly Jones, Joseph Habersham, and Edward Telfair, broke into the public powder magazine and made off with about five hundred pounds of gunpowder.

With word of the outbreak of hostilities, the tide turned in Georgia, and it turned abruptly and with increasing force against Governor Wright. In a matter of days, public feeling

28. Joseph Clay & Co. to Michael Collins, Apr. 8, 1775, Letter Book of Joseph Clay & Co., Ga. Hist. Soc.
29. Cowper & Telfair to Edward Telfair & Co., July 1, 1775, Edward Telfair Papers, Duke.
30. Wright to Dartmouth, Apr. 24, May 1, 2, 1775, unpub. Col. Records, XXXVIII, Part 1, 424-29, 431-32, 437.
31. Joseph Clay & Co. to Capt. Benjamin Mason, May 3, 1775, Letter Book of Joseph Clay & Co., Ga. Hist. Soc.

was obviously running strongly to the side of Liberty.[32]   The initiative now belonged to the Sons of Liberty.   On May 2, Wright had written that he was "very hopefull that no Unlawfull Restraint on Trade, or Violence will be Attempted in this Province."[33]   Three weeks later he wrote, "And to be Plain my Lord I see Nothing but a Prospect of a General Rebellion."[34] And by August, his government had disappeared in all but name.

Obviously the shots fired at Concord and Lexington echoed loud in Georgia, but the Liberty leaders did not immediately realize the magnitude of the consequent shift in public opinion.[35] Besides, the Liberty Boys still had their work cut out for them before Georgia would be firmly on the side of Liberty.   Their task was threefold: they had to stir up the apathetic and indifferent by words and deeds; they had to muster the force needed to intimidate the reluctant and to drive away or silence the hostile and then to wrest control from Governor Wright; and finally, they had to develop an organization capable of taking over the functions of the Wright-controlled government. There was nothing haphazard in the way the Liberty leaders went about attaining these objectives.   They fitted their plans to changing circumstances and took advantage of opportunities as they arose, but they worked toward their goals with a single-mindedness, not to say ruthlessness, that was impressive.

The Liberty leaders soon found something perhaps even more effective for arousing excitement than the fighting in New

32. Anthony Stokes, *A Narrative of the Official Conduct of Anthony Stokes* . . . (London, 1784), 8; Wright to Dartmouth, May 12, 1775, unpub. Col. Records, XXXVIII, Part 1, 439; *Ga. Gaz.*, May 17, 1775.

33. Wright to Dartmouth, May 2, 1775, unpub. Col. Records, XXXVIII, Part 1, 437.

34. Wright to Dartmouth, May 25, 1775, *ibid.*, 444-45.

35. On May 16, 1775, Joseph Clay, one of the leaders of the Liberty party, wrote to his associates, Bright and Pechin, in Philadelphia: "We have nothing New here at Present Marketts are much as usual" (Letter Book of Joseph Clay & Co., Ga. Hist. Soc.).   On the same day, Noble W. Jones, one of the more violent of the revolutionists, wrote to Benjamin Franklin apologizing for Georgia's not appearing "outwardly forward . . . thro some Tools of Administration" (Noble Wimberly Jones Papers, Duke University Library).

England, which, after all, was faraway. A report propagated in Charleston that the British planned to send troops to South Carolina and Georgia to arm the slaves and turn them loose on their masters threw the people of both provinces "into a Ferment."[36] There was talk both in Charleston and in Savannah of raising a colonial army. At about the same time, in late May, the stupidity of a government official in London provided the Liberty Boys with a new talking point, this time for building up resentment against Sir James Wright. An official letter of Wright's containing uncomplimentary references to the various meetings and congresses in America had been published in England and sent to Charleston. So great was the resentment in South Carolina when the letter was read there that several of Wright's friends wrote him about plans in the making for the Charleston Liberty Boys to come to Savannah and take him prisoner. Leaders in the Georgia Liberty party assured Wright of their disapproval of this project, but officers of the militia admitted that they could not answer for their men if called upon to protect the Governor.[37] Wright, of course, had personal enemies in the colony, and undoubtedly the publication of this letter fanned the feeling against him; but he always maintained there were many high in the councils of the Liberty party who were friendly to him to the end.

Early in June, the Savannah Liberty Boys found another occasion to stir up excitement, dramatize the growing power of the Liberty party and the dwindling influence of the Governor, and at the same time frighten a number of their enemies. On Friday, June 2, a small armed schooner came up the river to Savannah. To show their lack of regard for this addition to the Governor's strength, the Liberty Boys went that night to the battery at the east end of town, spiked the guns, and rolled them down the bluff. With the help of a number of the townspeople and sailors in port, Governor Wright got the

36. Wright to Dartmouth, May 25, 1775, unpub. Col. Records, XXXVIII, Part 1, 444-45.
37. Wright to Dartmouth, June 9, 1775, *ibid.*, 446-49.

guns remounted and enough bored out to fire a respectable number on Sunday, June 4, in celebration of the King's birthday. After the salute, the Governor, accompanied by several councilors and local gentlemen, "repaired to the flag staff to drink his Majesty's health," but the usual festivities were deferred until the next day.

On Monday, "his Excellency gave a genteel entertainment at the Court-House to the Members of the Council and Assembly, the Publick Officers, Officers of the Militia, and several other Gentlemen." A number of the assemblymen chose to forego the Governor's hospitality in order to join with the Liberty Boys in an entertainment of a slightly different sort. Out of the courthouse window the Governor's guests could see the Liberty Boys in the square as they erected the colony's first Liberty pole. At their dinner that evening in the long room of Tondee's tavern, the gentlemen of the Liberty party drank one toast to the King and many to various friends and slogans of Liberty, thus putting those gentlemen dining with the Governor under the unpleasant necessity of having their conversation punctuated by the "discharge of cannon placed under the Liberty flag" as each toast to Liberty was drunk. Although the Liberty Boys reportedly concluded their evening "with great decorum," they found time on their way home to parade about the town with fixed bayonets and to give four recent arrivals in Savannah a warning to get out of the province before the end of the week.[38]

The campaign of intimidation had by now been going on for several weeks, but this was the first time the Liberty Boys had made use of a mob to frighten their opponents. There had been one unrelated outbreak of mob violence earlier, in February, after the collector of the customs at Savannah had seized a shipment of untaxed molasses and foreign sugar on the river and stored it in the schooner *St. Johns* under the guard of his waiter and two seamen. On the night following, at about

38. *Ga. Gaz.*, June 7, 1775.

midnight, twenty or thirty men, armed and faces blackened, slipped down to the wharf where the ship was tied up and tarred and feathered the waiter, dumped the molasses into the river, and tossed the two seamen in after it. Since nothing was ever again heard of one of the seamen, there was "great Reason to believe that, not being permitted to come out of the River, he there perished and was drowned."[39]

But this apparently was an isolated instance. The so-called mob that appeared on the Savannah streets in the summer was of another sort. On June 5, it had not brought its tar pot and feathers along, and it chose for its victims men who were not permanent residents of the town; but the Liberty leaders were not again to show such discrimination and restraint, for thereafter they used the mob as an instrument of policy, a calculated policy of limited violence and terror directed toward the destruction of royal government. To bring about Wright's overthrow, his opponents accepted the necessity of resorting to force, and the only force available to them was a band of armed men which came to be known as the Savannah mob. Joseph Habersham, the young son of the president of the Council, James Habersham, who was at this time heartsick and dying, was the acknowledged leader of the Savannah mob and later became an effective enforcement agent for the council of safety. Composed for the most part of young gentlemen, laborers, and the town rowdies, the mob enabled the leaders of the revolutionary movement to intimidate Wright's supporters and hasten the collapse of his government.

By early June, the Liberty Boys' threats and defiance of authority were having effect. "There are Still many Friends to Government here," Wright declared on June 9, "but they begin to think they are left to Fall a Sacrifice to the Resentment of the People, for want of proper support & Protection And for their own Safety & other Prudential Reasons, are falling

39. *S. C. Gaz.; And Country Jour.*, Mar. 7, 1775.

off & lessening every day."[40]   Sir James requested that he be allowed to return to England.

The local Sons of Liberty reassembled in Savannah on June 13, ostensibly to assure that the four proscribed strangers had left the province.   Some three or four hundred strong, they put up a Liberty tree and during the evening paraded about the town.   The real business at hand was the organizing of the party's fast-expanding power.   The party leaders had first abandoned the old government, then, by threats and violence, had undermined it and demonstrated its incapacity.   Now, "convinced of the necessity of preventing the anarchy and confusion which attend the dissolution of the powers of government," they, like good revolutionists, were seeking to take control under pretense of rescuing what they had in fact destroyed.[41]   At Tondee's tavern, the leaders of the Liberty party outlined what was to be done to replace Wright's regime with their own.   They began by pledging to give the directives of the Continental Congress the force of law in Christ's Church parish.   A parochial committee for enforcing the directives in the parish was to be appointed at a meeting set for June 22.   This committee was promised the strong support and complete obedience of the Savannah Sons of Liberty.   Before breaking up, the Savannah meeting recommended its resolutions to the other parishes and called for a provincial congress to meet at Savannah on July 4 so that the entire province could be organized under radical leadership.[42]   Unlike the opposition to the Stamp Act which had come mainly from the country, the leadership of the revolutionary movement in Georgia centered

40. Wright to Dartmouth, June 9, 1775, unpub. Col. Records, XXXVIII, Part 1, 446-49.

41. *Ga. Gaz.*, June 14, 1775.

42. *Ibid.;* Wright to Dartmouth, June 17, 1775, Ga. Hist. Soc., *Colls.,* III, 183-85.   At the meeting held on June 22, a parochial council of safety was formed with William Ewen, president, Seth John Cuthbert, secretary, and Joseph Habersham, Edward Telfair, William Le Conte, Basil Cowper, Joseph Clay, George Walton, John Glen, Samuel Elbert, William Young, Elisha Butler, George Houstoun, John Smith, Francis H. Harris, and John Morel. Stevens, *History of Georgia*, II, 101.

about the town of Savannah where merchants such as Edward Telfair, Basil Cowper, Seth John Cuthbert, and Joseph Clay were much more active than they had been in 1766.

Before their next meeting the Sons of Liberty got another justification for arming men and another issue with which to stir up the populace. It was South Carolina once again that caused the excitement. The Sons of Liberty of that province put out the report that John Stuart, long-time superintendent of Indian affairs, had been trying to instigate a Cherokee attack on the whites of South Carolina. Stuart, who fled from Charleston to Savannah about the middle of June with the Carolinians in hot pursuit, found Savannah little more cordial and put to sea in a schooner bound for St. Augustine. Several boats conveying perhaps fifty to eighty armed men came into the mouth of the Savannah River from Carolina with the announced purpose of seizing Stuart. Governor Wright suspected that they were in reality more interested in waylaying the *Philippa,* a ship then due from England with a large cargo of gunpowder aboard. This proved to be the case. The "Liberty Gentlemen" of Georgia fitted out a schooner and joined the South Carolinians in their vigil off Tybee Island. In early July, the *Philippa* appeared and was made to come to off the bar. It was then conducted up to Cockspur Island where Joseph Habersham and his men went aboard and took off about six tons of powder which they divided with the Carolinians.[43]

All during the month of June, Governor Wright could do little but stand helplessly by as his power crumbled. He still had no troops. Both he and the Council had decided the one hundred men promised would be worse than none at all. Any less than five hundred, they feared, would only serve to enrage the people and give rise to new outbreaks of violence. Wright felt that nothing less than a warship stationed in the river and a fort built on the town common would allow him to weather

43. Wright to Dartmouth, June 20, July 8, 1775, Ga. Hist. Soc., *Colls.,* III, 189-90, 191-92; Deposition of Richard Maitland, Master of the *Philippa,* Sept. 21, 1775, unpub. Col. Records, XXXVIII, Part 1, 606-16.

the storm.⁴⁴   His letters to General Gage and to Admiral
Graves outlining his predicament and asking that ships be sent
were intercepted by the committee in Charleston which substituted clumsily forged letters assuring the British commanders
that all was quiet in Georgia.   Significantly, in both letters
Governor Wright expressed almost as much interest in news
as in reinforcements; he had found that any report of British
success had the effect of bolstering up his wavering followers
and of putting a damper on the Liberty Boys.⁴⁵

On the morning of July 4, the day that the provincial
congress convened, the sad state to which the power and influence of the Royal Governor had fallen was made plain.   At
about eleven o'clock, Joseph Habersham and several others
showed up at the filature in Savannah and calmly began loading the colony's store of munitions onto a horse-drawn cart.
The commissary general went to Governor Wright, who was
in council, and told him what was happening.   Wright instructed the commissary to go and tell them "to desist" at once.
The loading party, taking no notice of Wright's order except to
assure the commissary that they were keeping a list of what they
took, continued to cart the guns and supplies down to the river
and onto a waiting schooner with pointed deliberateness.⁴⁶

The second provincial congress met in Savannah on July 4
and put an end to any illusions that the government of Sir
James Wright still ruled in Georgia.   The provincial congress,
with Archibald Bulloch as president and George Walton as
secretary, immediately became the *de facto* legislature of the
colony with the committee of correspondence, and later the
council of safety, its executive.   Georgia promptly ranged herself alongside her sister colonies in revolt and chose delegates
to the Continental Congress.   Sir James was too old a hand not

44. Wright to Dartmouth, June 17, 1775, Ga. Hist. Soc., *Colls.*, III, 187-88.
45. Wright to General Gage, June 27, 1775, unpub. Col. Records, XXXVIII,
Part 2, 26-28; Wright to Admiral Graves, June 27, 1775, *ibid.*, 29-31.
46. Deposition of George Baillie, Commissary General, July 5, 1775, *ibid.*,
XXXVIII, Part 1, 497-98.

to be fully aware of what had happened to him. While the congress was in session, he wrote Dartmouth: "The Powers of Government are wrested out of my Hands . . . Law & Government are nearly if not quite annihilated."[47]

For six months more Wright remained in Georgia and watched with horror, despair, and indignation as the revolutionists completed the destruction of his government and consolidated their power. Control of the militia passed out of his hands in July and the law courts in December. The end did not in fact come until his arrest by Joseph Habersham on January 18, 1776, and his subsequent flight in February to H. M. S. *Scarborough*; but after July 4, 1775, the story of Georgia was no longer Wright's. He returned in the summer of 1779 after the British capture of Savannah and acted as Royal Governor for three more years. The effectiveness of his administration and the extent of his jurisdiction during these years of strife and bloodshed were determined by the military might, or lack of it, of British forces in the area at any given time. In July 1782, James Wright set sail from Savannah for the last time as the town was evacuated and Georgia began its experiment with independence.

How the revolutionists finally overpowered Governor Wright in 1775 and brought Georgia in on the side of the American colonies against Britain is fairly plain. The *why* of it is much less clear. By all counts, the people in general followed where they were led, most bowing to the superior force of the Liberty Boys or responding naturally to the passions and hurrah of the moment. The leaders, both rebel and tory, were all, or practically all, merchants and planters who together composed the dominant class of the colony. Later, after the coming of invasion and civil war to Georgia, the revolutionary movement developed overtones of sectional and class conflict; but in the summer of crisis of 1775 there was little evidence of either. More than one merchant or planter

47. Wright to Dartmouth, July 8, 1775, Ga. Hist. Soc., *Colls.*, III, 192.

trimmed his sails to the wind, leaning toward rebellion when the Savannah mob roamed and toward loyalty when British troops held the upper hand. But many a rebel and tory displayed deep conviction and stubborn courage from beginning to end. Why was one man a convinced rebel and his brother or neighbor a convinced tory? Why was Edward Telfair a revolutionist and his brother William a loyalist? Why did the Houstouns, the Habershams, the Joneses, the Gibbonses, the Farleys, divide in their loyalties, some in a family going one way and some the other? The ultimate answer could be arrived at only through an intimate understanding of each man—of his native temperament, of his way of thinking, of his ideas and ideals, aspirations, and private circumstances. But there is a pattern of sorts, vague, blurred in outline, and contradictory though it is. A man who was a royal official was, for obvious reasons, usually a loyalist to the end. A merchant or planter who became a rebel was more likely to be American-born than English, more likely a Scottish Highlander than a Salzburger, and likelier a St. Johns Congregationalist than either. And the rebel leader was ordinarily younger than his tory counterpart.

The question remains why a large segment of the ruling group in Georgia chose to lead the colony into revolt, for in 1775 the merchants and planters of Georgia had no serious economic grievance to solidify or embitter them as a class. Times were good, better than ever. Even nature seemed to conspire to keep them happy with bumper rice crops. Most had prospered far beyond what they could have hoped. All but a few had come to Georgia with little or no capital and by 1775 many were well-to-do or on the way to becoming so. The promotion of their economic welfare had long been the main concern of the royal governor, and in this new country the advantages of belonging to the mercantile system of the Empire had always far outweighed, and still did, any restrictions it imposed. Certainly Georgia was not led into revolution by men enraged at the workings of malignant economic forces.

Nor was the pressure for independence entirely political in the conventional sense. The merchants and planters of Georgia had enjoyed good government under Governor Ellis and Governor Wright. They had been given a strong voice in its councils; royal government had brought with it new political power and responsibility to the colonist of substance. It is true that after 1765 the elected assembly had chafed under the domination of Governor Wright and through the years had bitterly disputed with him over points of prerogative. The Assembly's persistent aims were to enlarge the sphere of colonial self-government and to restrict the sphere of the royal governor. But this is not revolution. It is a story as old as America itself, as old as the story of representative government or of imperial relationships on this earth—the people against their masters, the legislature against the executive, colony against mother country.

This struggle for power which had been part and parcel of America's development from the beginning became revolutionary in the 1770's when enough Americans and their leaders came to believe that Britain was taking away their fundamental rights, leaving them only the choice between submission to tyranny or independence, that self-government in the individual colonies was being threatened by King and Parliament, and that the policy of the mother country had become to enrich herself without due regard for the interests of her colonies. Georgia was a part of the British Empire, and any threat to the other colonies was in the long run a threat to Georgia. To a greater or lesser degree the rebels of Georgia trembled for their liberties like the rest; but to transform this fear into a determination to fight required of the Georgians a greater act of imagination than was required of the other colonists. What the merchants and planters of Georgia were being asked to do was nothing less than to reject the advantages of explosive prosperity and rapid expansion under the patently invaluable leadership of Sir James Wright for a set of principles which still remained, for Georgians, largely abstractions.

It is hardly credible that Georgia, left alone, would have made the decision she did. Had the Savannah River been fifty miles wide instead of only a few yards, the people of Georgia would hardly have even considered breaking with Britain in 1776. Governor Wright insisted loud and long that his overthrow was due to the evil influence of the other colonies upon his charge. Although there was in this something of the parent who blames the nastiness of his child on the bad example set by the children of his neighbor, he had a point. Exposed to the heat of passion, Georgia burst into flame. When it hung back in the spring of 1775, many in Georgia had a feeling of being left out, of not having a part in great events. For the Liberty people it seemed intolerable, shameful even, that the other colonies should show the courage to stand up for colonial rights while Georgia did nothing. The people of Georgia when they chose independence were not so much rejecting the old as reaching out for the new. Georgia was borne into the Revolution by forces from the outside which, by their strength and wide compass, swept aside local and personal considerations, leaving the conviction that Georgia needs must share the fate of the rest of America.

All that Henry Ellis and James Wright did to build up the colony, and they did much, had the ultimate effect of increasing the self-confidence and ambition of the merchant-planter class in Georgia. The arrival of thousands of new settlers, the great and continuing increase in production and trade, the lessening of the colony's dependence upon Britain for protection against the Indians only served to make it easier for the merchants and planters first to oppose the Governor and then to revolt. Farms, plantations, and towns where in 1754 there had been only swamp and forest were the monuments of royal government Sir James Wright left behind in 1776; but the final measure of his and Ellis's success, and the success of royal government, was that the men who had learned the art of government under English rule could build in the 1780's on the ruins of the old a new government founded on law and given stability by the acceptance of its people. The story of the royal governor in Georgia is a success story. The revolt in 1776 does not spoil it. If the royal governor helped sow the seeds of rebellion, it was not because he failed but because he succeeded too well.

Bibliographical Note

Bibliographical Note

MAIN RELIANCE for an investigation of the royal period of Georgia's history must of necessity be upon that mass of official papers known as the Colonial Records. These records consist of material relating to the colony of Georgia in the Public Record Office, London, transcripts of which were obtained by the state at the turn of this century. Between 1904 and 1916 the state, under the editorship of Allen D. Candler and his successor Lucian L. Knight, published at Atlanta twenty-six volumes with the title *The Colonial Records of the State of Georgia*. In addition to these Governor Candler edited three volumes called *The Revolutionary Records of the State of Georgia* (Atlanta, 1908). Lilla M. Hawes has added to the published official record by editing for the *Georgia Historical Quarterly* the "Proceedings of the President and Assistants in Council of Georgia, 1749-1751," Part 1, XXXV (December 1951) and Part 2, XXXVI (March 1952). Published in the *Collections of the Georgia Historical Society*, III (Savannah, 1873), are "Letters from Sir James Wright," containing a number of his official letters, and in Volume X (Savannah, 1952), *The Proceedings and Minutes of the Governor and Council of Georgia, October 4, 1774, through November 7, 1775, and September 6, 1779, through September 20, 1780*, edited by Lilla M. Hawes. There are also published the *Journal of the Congress of the Four Southern Governors, and the Superintendent of that District, with the Five Nations of Indians, at Augusta, 1763* (Charleston, 1764), and *Historical*

Collections of Georgia (New York, 1854), by George White.

Much of the transcript made in London remains unpublished, however, including most of the official correspondence of the royal governors, the single most important source of information for this study. Fortunately, typescript copies of these unpublished Colonial Records have been made and deposited at the University of Georgia Library, Athens; the State Department of Archives and History, Atlanta; and the Georgia Historical Society Library, Savannah. Additional official and semi-official correspondence of each of the three governors is to be found in the William Henry Lyttelton Papers, William L. Clements Library, Ann Arbor, Michigan; Thomas Gage Papers, American Series, Clements Library; and Jeffrey Amherst Papers, Library of Congress.

Second in importance only to the published and unpublished Colonial Records as a source of information are the newspapers of the time. Most important, of course, is the colony's only newspaper, *The Georgia Gazette,* published at Savannah from 1763 (with brief interruptions) through the remainder of the colonial period. Almost as useful are the files of *The South-Carolina Gazette,* Charleston. Valuable items relating to Georgia during these years are also to be found in *The South-Carolina Gazette; And Country Journal,* Charleston, and *The Pennsylvania Gazette,* Philadelphia, as well as in *The London Magazine* and *The London Chronicle: or, Universal Evening Post.*

With the exception of a fairly substantial, and very valuable, collection of letters published in the *Collections of the Georgia Historical Society,* VI (Savannah, 1904), under the title of *The Letters of Hon. James Habersham, 1756-1775,* there is a dearth of papers left by the colonials themselves. The Raymond Demeré Papers, the Edward Telfair Papers, the Gibbons Papers, the George Walton Papers, and the Noble W. Jones Papers in the Duke University Library contain few items, except for the Gibbons-Telfair Papers. The last, taken together with the Edward Telfair Letter Books that are to be found in Savannah, comprises an excellent and largely unexploited source for mercantile and agricultural developments in Georgia during the last half of the eighteenth century and the first half of the nineteenth. The Rasberry Letter Book and the Letter Book of Joseph Clay & Co., April 11, 1774, to May 16, 1776, both in the Georgia Historical Society Library, and *Letters of Joseph Clay Merchant of Savannah 1776-1793*, published in *Collections of the Georgia Historical Society*, VIII (Savannah, 1913), contain further data in connection with mercantile operations. Except for the Midway Congregational Church Records, 1754-1788, Georgia Historical Society Library, and Bonds, Bills of Sale, Deeds of Gift, Powers of Attorney: 1765, September 5–1772, March 5, Georgia Department of Archives and History, Atlanta, little other pertinent manuscript material survives.

There are, however, a number of invaluable published works written by participants in the events of pre-Revolutionary Georgia: engineer John Gerar William De Brahm's *History of the Province of Georgia* (Wormsloe, Ga., 1849); John Bartram's *Diary of a Journey Through the Carolinas, Georgia, and Florida: From July 1, 1765, to April 10, 1766*, in *Transactions of the American Philosophical Society*, New Series, XXXIII, Part I (Philadelphia, 1942); Governor Henry Ellis's, *A Voyage to Hudson's-Bay, by the Dobbs Galley and California, in the Years 1746 and 1747, for Discovering a North West Passage* (Dublin, 1749), first published in London in 1748; Chief Justice Anthony Stokes' *A View of the Constitution of the British Colonies, in North-America and the West-Indies, at the Time the Civil War Broke Out on the Continent of America . . .* (London, 1783) and his *A Narrative of the Official Conduct of Anthony Stokes . . .* (London, 1784). Captain Hugh McCall's *The History of Georgia containing Brief Sketches of the Most Remarkable Events Up to the Present Day (1784)* (Atlanta,

1909), first published in 1811, although for the most part rather inferior history, has the advantage of being written soon after the event, as do John Nichols' *Literary Anecdotes of the Eighteenth Century* (London, 1812-1815), Volume IX, and *Illustrations of the Literary History of the Eighteenth Century* (London, 1817-1858), Volume I, both of which provide information about Governor Henry Ellis's career after his departure from Georgia in 1760.

Although I have cited but few books and articles of scholars who have worked the field before me, it is not because I have not learned much from them or because I do not recognize their achievements. I have cut off for investigation a segment of the colony's history, and much of the writing on colonial Georgia falls outside these limits. Also, the decision to view the period from a stance differing from previous accounts necessitated going back to the records. The most careful and complete account that we have of the royal period (*A History of Georgia from Its First Discovery by Europeans to the Adoption of the Present Constitution in MDCCXCVIII*, Volume II [Philadelphia, 1859]) was done by Bishop William Bacon Stevens, the passionate whig historian of the nineteenth century and the state's most distinguished until the appearance of E. Merton Coulter. Following Stevens, Charles C. Jones, Jr., wrote a two-volume *History of Georgia* (Boston, 1883), and Percy Scott Flippin's study of royal government in Georgia published in the *Georgia Historical Quarterly* (1924-29) remains valuable. In this century, Professor Coulter and Albert B. Saye have for the most part written about the earlier period of settlement when they have turned their attention to colonial history. Alexander A. Lawrence, the most knowledgeable and productive scholar interested in this period, has published excellent studies of James Johnston and Anthony Stokes, both important figures of the time. And Alex M. Hitz has written a revealing study of the Wrightsborough Quaker town and township in the *Bulletin of Friends Historical Association,* XLVI, 1957. Kenneth Coleman's *Georgia in the American Revolution, 1763-1789* (Athens, Ga., 1958) is being published as this book goes to press.

Index

Index